JOSHUA

"WE WILL SERVE THE LORD"

by

Cyril J. Barber

A DEVOTIONAL EXPOSITION

Wipf & Stock
PUBLISHERS
Eugene, Oregon

Scripture quotations have been taken from the
Holy Bible, New International Version.
Copyrighted (c) 1973, 1978, 1984
by the International Bible Society.
Used by permission of Zondervan Publishing House.
All rights reserved.
Scripture quotations have also been taken from the
New King James Version of the Bible.
(c) 1979, 1980, 1982, by Thomas Nelson, Inc., Publishers.
Used by permission of Thomas Nelson Publishers.
All rights reserved.
And scripture quotations have been taken from the
New American Standard Bible
(c) 1960, 1962, 1963, 1968, 1971, 1972, 1973,
1975, and 1977
by the Lockman Foundation, and are used
by permission.

Paraphrases of Scripture are the author's.

Biblical references in parentheses (e.g., 6:5)
are to the Book of Joshua.

Wipf and Stock Publishers
199 W 8th Ave, Suite 3
Eugene, OR 97401

Joshua
A Devotional Exposition
By Barber, Cyril J.
Copyright©2006 by Barber, Cyril J.
ISBN: 1-59752-552-9
Publication date 2/1/2006

This book is inscribed with affection and
gratitude to
Celia Sundin and Jan Hussey
Whose work in the office of Plymouth Church
often goes unnoticed.

And to the Deaconesses of Plymouth Church;
Sharon Cahn (chair),
Aldyth Barber, Jo Blue, Janet Boulter,
Inez Commander, Mary Lou De La Torre,
Lorraine Hover, Lorraine McGee,
Katy Linklater, Cindy Marsden,
Kathy Schreiber,
Barbara Smith, Beverlee Smith,
and Audrey Wagg
Whose indefatigable labors behind the scenes
are deeply appreciated.

And to our custodian,
Ernie Ortiz
Without whose help nothing would
run smoothly.

CONTENTS

PREFACE
INTRODUCTION

1 THE GIFT OF THE LAND (1:1-9) 1
2 THE MISSION OF THE SPIES (2:1-24) 15
3 CROSSING THE RIVER JORDAN, Pt. 1 (3:1–4:24) 31
4 CROSSING THE RIVER JORDAN, Pt. 2 (3:1–4:24) 43
5 PREPARING FOR CONQUEST (5:1-15). 53
6 THE CAPTURE OF JERICHO (6:1-27) 63
7 RESTORING GOD'S FAVOR (7:1-26) 73
8 THE CAPTURE OF AI (8:1-35) 89
9 THE CONQUEST OF SOUTHERN CANAAN, ... 101
  Pt. 1 (9:1–10:43)
10 THE CONQUEST OF SOUTHERN CANAAN, ... 113
   Pt. 2 (10:1-43)
11 CONQUEST OF NORTHERN CANAAN (11:1-15) 127
12 THE DIVISION OF THE LAND, Pt 1 (13:1–21:45) 141
13 THE DIVISION OF THE LAND, Pt. 2 (13:1–21:45) 151
14 JOSHUA'S FAREWELL MESSAGES Pt. 1 (22:1-34) ... 163
15 JOSHUA'S FAREWELL MESSAGES, Pt. 2 (23:1-16) .. 175
16 JOSHUA'S FAREWELL MESSAGES, Pt. 3 (24:1-28) .. 185

PREFACE

In 1974 I submitted *Nehemiah and the Dynamics of Effective Leadership* to Loizeaux Brothers for publication. They liked my work and the editor, Miss Marie Loizeaux, asked me to write a series of commentaries covering Judges through 2 Chronicles to fill a gap left by the great Bible expositor, the late Dr. Harry Ironside. This was a considerable honor, for I have limitless admiration for Dr. Ironside and do not believe for one moment that any contribution of mine could equal his! In acquiescing to Marie's request I spent the next twenty-five years completing the assignment she gave me. Unfortunately, after a long and distinguished history spanning more than one hundred and twenty years, Loizeaux Brothers ceased publication and all of their books went out of print in a single day.

Dr. Ironside had written a discerning work on Joshua, and so readers might well ask the reason for the present monograph. Though some of Dr. Ironside's commentaries have been reprinted, at the present time his *Joshua* is no longer available. This led some of my good friends to suggest that I produce a work that might meet the need of contemporary Bible students.

I prayed over this suggestion and gradually the prospect of writing on Joshua took hold. I have had a longstanding fascination with the Book of Joshua. What has impressed me is the place of God's Word in the life of a godly leader, and the trustworthiness of God in fulfilling to the letter all His promises.

The Hebrew Bible (comprising the Law, *the Prophets*, and the Writings) forms an indispensable backdrop to a meaningful study of the New Testament. *The Prophets* are divided into two sections: "The Former Prophets" (Joshua through 2 Kings) and "The Latter Prophets" (Isaiah through Malachi). With the absence of Dr. Ironside's work on Joshua there is a need for a devotional exposition to complete this portion of the Old Testament. But isn't the term "The Former Prophets" out of place when reference is made to books that are largely historical? *The ancient Hebrews gave these books the title of "The Former Prophets" because they believed that these canonical works had been written under the prompting of the Spirit of God.*

It is with the firm belief that the Book of Joshua is a part of inspired Scripture that I have undertaken this exposition. When I penned my earlier works I provided my own translation of the Hebrew text. This is no longer possible for my failing eyesight greatly limits my ability. The chapters that follow are designed for lay people. They are simple and unsophisticated. I have left critical matters to those whose abilities far exceed my own.

In closing I would like to express my deep gratitude to my dear friends Maurice Bickley and David Cahn for their help in preparing the manuscript for publication.

May the Lord use this brief explanation of the scope of the Book of Joshua as He sees fit!

INTRODUCTION

In introducing readers to the important features of the Book of Joshua the late Dr. Francis A. Schaeffer wrote: "Joshua is an important book for many reasons–for the history it records and for its internal teaching. But what makes the book of Joshua overwhelmingly important is that it stands as a bridge, a link between the Pentateuch (the writings of Moses) and the rest of Scripture. It is crucial to understanding the unity the Pentateuch has with all that follows it, including the New Testament."[1]

Criticism of the Book. Controversy surrounds the Book of Joshua, and liberal critics of the Bible have seized upon the issues of the book's historical setting, ethics (e.g., Rahab's lie, and the destruction of the Canaanites), inclusion of miracles (the parting of the waters of the River Jordan, the collapse of the walls of Jericho), as well as the authorship and date, to minimize the value of what God has chosen to reveal.[2] In spite of their attacks what is recorded provides an authoritative account of the faithfulness of God in fulfilling the promises He had made to the Patriarchs (21:43-45).

---

1. F. A. Schaeffer, *Joshua and the Flow of Biblical History* (Downers Grove, IL: InterVarsity, 1975), 9. Introductory matters have been discussed at length by the great Scottish preacher and teacher, William G. Blaikie, in his *Book of Joshua* (Minneapolis, MN: Klock and Klock, 1978), 1-36.

It has often been asked, How could God bless Rahab for lying? In answering this charge it should be pointed out that God did not bless Rahab's lie, He did honor her faith. Her act in protecting the spies was a demonstration of her faith in the God of Israel. Rahab serves as an example of justified civil disobedience. Of course, had she been found out her life would have been terminated in a most cruel way!

Other critics claim that archaeology demonstrates the biblical account of the taking of Jericho to be inaccurate. Though Jericho was an exceedingly ancient city, Dr. Kathleen Kenyon (who excavated the ancient site) claimed that it ceased to exist around 1550 B.C. This, of course, was almost a century and a half before the Israelites invaded Canaan. Professor Kenyon's position was shown to be in error by Bryant G. Wood whose article in the March/April, 1990, edition of the *Biblical Archaeology Review* proves conclusively that the biblical record is accurate.

It also has been argued that the total destruction of the Canaanites and Amorites is morally unjustifiable. As we

---

2. For a discussion, more lengthy and complex than is possible here, see G. L. Archer, Jr., *A Survey of Old Testament Introduction* (Chicago: Moody, 1994), 285-99; R. B. Dillard and T. Longman, III, *An Introduction to the Old Testament* (Grand Rapids: Zondervan, 1994), 107-17; R. K. Harrison, *Introduction to the Old Testament* (Grand Rapids: Eerdmans, 1969), 665-79; A. E. Hill and J. H. Walton, *A Survey of the Old Testament* (Grand Rapids: Zondervan, 1991), 161-72; and D. M. Howard, Jr., *An Introduction to the Old Testament Historical Books* (Chicago: Moody, 1993), 59-98. Books of this nature are legion, and readers are encouraged to consult their local theological library.

place this issue in the light of history, we find that these races were far from innocent. Leviticus 18 describes their sins (note vv. 21, 24-26), and in Genesis 15:16 we learn that the Lord gave the people 400 years to repent. Israel, therefore, became God's rod to chasten the people of the land.

But was it right to punish the children as well? God is merciful, and children who die before the age of accountability are not condemned along with those who have sinned against the light God had given them (cf. 2 Samuel 12:23).

Issues such as the crossing of the River Jordan, the destruction of Jericho, and Joshua's "long day" will be treated in the exposition with other data being confined to the footnotes.

Interpretation of the Text. Many who represent extreme right-wing conservatives, have approached the Book of Joshua as an allegory of the spiritual life. They believe that the events were true historically, but of greater interest to them are the parallels between the actual experiences of the Israelites and the spiritual experiences of God's people today.

The approach adopted here, is to follow the literal, critical, and cultural approach to hermeneutics, and see in the Book of Joshua God's gift of land to His chosen people. As such the book is transitional. Principles of application may then be drawn from the text.

Authorship

The titles given many of the writings of the Old Testament focus, for the most part, on their subject matter rather than on the author. With the Book of Joshua, however, we encounter for the first time a work that bears the name of the principal character. But was Joshua also the author? This issue has been debated *ad nauseam* with some critics assigning the book a date in the reign of Josiah. Internal evidence, however, points to the fact that the book was composed by an eyewitness. It is true that some sections (e.g., 15:13-17; 24:29-33) could not have been written by Joshua, but these could easily have been supplied by Eleazar the priest or by Phinehas his son. And in favor of Joshua's authorship is the fact that much of the book contains the record of someone who participated in the events. This is evident from the fact that in 5:1 the writer uses "we" and in 5:6 "us." Finally, in 24:1-26 Joshua is specifically identified as the author.

The authorship of the book is tied in with the date of the events that are recorded. The use of the phrase "to this day" (4:9; 5:9; 7:26; 8:28; etc.) indicates that the book was written shortly after the events described. This, too, would support the book having been written by Joshua (perhaps with the scribal help of his amanuenses).

Date

The writing of the book of Joshua is intimately connected with the entrance of the Israelites into Canaan. The biblical evidence indicates that the exodus from Egypt took place around 1446 B.C., with the conquest of the land beginning about 40 years later. Two lines of evidence confirm this date. First Kings 6:1 indicates that the building of the Temple in Jerusalem commenced in the year 967 B.C., 480 years after the descendants of Jacob came out of Egypt. A date for the Exodus around 1446 B.C. is highly probable. The journeys of the Israelites through the wilderness took approximately 40 years. This would place the tribes on the banks of the River Jordan around the year 1406 B.C.

The second line of evidence supports this conclusion. A statement made by Jephthah in Judges 11:26 refers to the fact that the Israelites had lived in Heshbon and its villages for 300 years prior to his judgship. Dr. Merrill F. Unger has calculated the time from Jephthah's judgship to the building of the Temple in the fourth year of Solomon's reign and found that it confirms a 1446 B.C. date for the Exodus. There seems to be no real reason, therefore, why the invasion of Canaan by the Israelites did not occur about the year 1406 B.C., and the Book of Joshua was most assuredly completed soon after the conquest of the land.[3]

Negative critics of the Bible place the date of the Exodus much later. Their views can be traced by consulting the introductions contained in critical Bible commentaries.[4]

---

3. See M. F. Unger, *Introductory Guide to the Old Testament* (Grand Rapids: Zondervan, 1951), 281-83, 89.
4. A thorough treatment of the issues is to be found in the excellent work by L. J. Wood, *A Survey of Israel's History*, revised by D. O'Brien (Grand Rapids: Zondervan, 1986), 65-86.

Outline of the Book

There are four main parts to the book of Joshua:
  I. The Invasion of the Land (1:1–5:15)
  II. The Conquest of the Land (6:1–12:24)
  III. The Distribution of the Land (13:1–21:45), and
  IV. Joshua's Concluding Exhortations and Death (22:1–24:33).

This initial outline will be enlarged as we tackle each section.

Who Was Joshua?

Who was Joshua, and why was he chosen to succeed Moses?

Joshua's name was originally *Hosea'*, but was changed by Moses to *Yehosua'*, meaning "Yahweh saves." In the Septuagint translation of the Old Testament into Greek his name is given as *Iesous*.

The ancient Hebrews prided themselves on their ancestry, and certainly they still have an enviable heritage. In the case of Joshua, however, he could trace his lineage back to Joseph, and it was his ancestor Ephraim who was promised greater blessings than his brother (Genesis 48:1-22, noting esp. vv. 20-22; 1 Chronicles 7:20-29).

Though born in slavery, Joshua came from a distinguished family. His grandfather, Elishama (1 Chronicles 7:26) was the *rosh*, "head, leader" of his tribe (cf. Numbers 1:10, 2:18), and we can only imagine the influence this great man had on his son, Nun, and aspiring grandson, Joshua.

As Joshua grew toward manhood he took pride in his national heritage, and even the harsh treatment he and his fellow Hebrews received from the Egyptian taskmasters did not diminish his belief in his nation's God. And slavery, far from causing him to despair of God's goodness, developed in him an fervent expectation of deliverance.

In the course of time a deliverer came to God's people: Moses. A succession of miracles, known as the plagues of Egypt, convinced Pharaoh to let God's people go.[5] The march began and Joshua witnessed firsthand the parting of the Red Sea and the destruction of Pharaoh's army.

Joshua's grandfather, Elishama, marched at the head of the 45,000 men who made up the fighting force of the tribe of Ephraim.[6] The 2,000,000-plus Israelites who left Egypt under Moses were strung out over a considerable distance. Progress was slow because of the sheep and cattle that had

---

5. W. C. Kaiser, Jr., *A History of Israel* (Nashville: Broadman & Holman, 1998), 95-101.
6. Throughout the wilderness march the men of this tribe took particular care of Joseph's coffin (Exodus 13:19; cf. Joshua 24:32), for he had given specific instructions that his remains were to be laid to rest in Canaan.

to be herded in the right direction. And each household had to carry or push a cart containing all of their belongings.

The journey down the Sinai Peninsula seemed to have only just begun when wily Bedouin called Amalekites attacked the sick who brought up the rear (Exodus 17:8-16; cf. Deuteronomy 25:17-18). The place was Rephidim in the Wilderness of Sinai, and Joshua was chosen to repulse their attack.[7] The Israelites had no militia, and had not experienced war before.

Joshua showed no hesitation in accepting the charge, and though he had little time to prepare a strategy (for the Amalekites attacked again the next day), he and his men waged a fierce battle against them. Moses, as we know, stood on the top of a hill with the rod of God in his hand. This was the same rod that had been stretched out over the Red Sea, and as long as Moses held his arms up Joshua and his small band prevailed (Exodus 17:9-14). It was a memorable victory that showed Joshua to be a man of faith and courage. The modeling of these qualities by his grandfather and father was beginning to pay off.

After the Battle of Rephidim Moses selected Joshua to be his personal aide.

Once at the foot of Mount Sinai Moses, accompanied by Joshua, ascended the mountain (Exodus 24:13). Moses was enveloped by a cloud and communed with the Lord for forty days and forty nights. During all this time Joshua

---

7. Blaikie, *Joshua*, 24.

remained at a lower level. In this we see his patience, obedience and self-control. He did not go looking for Moses nor return to the camp, but waited confidently for Moses to return.

Of Joshua's patience Dr. William G. Blaikie wrote: "More than three thousand years have sped away, but have the servants of God on an average reached the measure of Joshua's patience? Prayers unanswered, promises unfulfilled, sickness protracted during weary years of pain, disappointments and trials coming in troops as if all God's waves and billows were passing over them, active persecution bringing all the devices of torture to bear upon them – how have such things tried the patience, the waiting power of the servants of God! But let them remember that if the trial be severe the recompense [will be] great."[8]

At last Moses returned, carrying the tablets with the Decalogue inscribed on them. As they approached the camp of Israel, they heard a noise that resembled the cries of battle. Moses reassured his youthful aide that what he heard was neither the sound of the victors nor of the vanquished, but a riotous bacchanalian frenzy. The people had made a golden calf and, having thrown off all restraints, were worshiping it in the most shameful and unholy way.

The contrast between the glory of God revealed on the top of Mount Sinai and the depraved and polluted passions of those in the camp could not be greater. Moses threw

---

8. Ibid., 29.

down the tablets of the Law and smashed them at the base of the mountain. In grace the Lord gave Moses another copy, and this copy was placed in the Tabernacle once it had been built.

Not long after the completion of the Tabernacle Joshua was given another important task. The Israelites had moved on and had camped at Kadesh-Barnea.[9] He and eleven other leaders, one man from each tribe, were sent to spy out the land of Canaan (Numbers 13:1–14:45). They went two-by-two through the land and brought back some of its produce. The report of Joshua and Caleb encouraged the Israelites to go up and possess the land. The report of the other ten spies was unfavorable, and they instilled fear into the hearts of their brethren. So fearful did the people become that they spoke of stoning Joshua and Caleb, and returning to Egypt. Joshua and Caleb were only saved from being stoned to death when the glory of the Lord appeared at the entrance to the Tabernacle. As punishment the ten spies died in a plague before the Lord that day, and all the Israelites twenty years of age and up were told that their unbelief would keep them out of the land God had promised to the Patriarchs.

---

9. See H. C. Trumbull, *Kadesh-Barnea: Its Importance and Probable Site* (London: Hodder & Stoughton, 1884), 478pp, plus map tracing the route of the Exodus. The probable site of Kadesh-Barnea is described on pages 272ff.

For thirty-eight years we hear nothing more of Joshua. When he emerges from obscurity, it is to lead the new generation into the land of promise.

With this brief resume before us, we do well to review the past and ask what abiding lessons we can draw from the experiences of this notable leader. First and foremost is the place of prayer in any successful endeavor. The fact that Moses held up his arms (symbolizing his prayers for his people) during the entire day of battle, gave Joshua and his army the victory. During this day Joshua and his band of untrained followers, so recently released from slavery, took on the formidable and warlike Amalekites. And they defeated them.

From the prayers of Moses we turn to consider Joshua's leadership qualities. Initially he must have been the kind of leader who could be looked up to and respected; whose personal judgment could be trusted, and who could inspire and warm the hearts of his followers, for the Israelites were no match for the desert hardened and well-trained Amalekites. To give incentive to his men Joshua's instructions must have had the ring of confidence. Sound leadership must be based on truth and character, and in Joshua's case it was founded upon his Godward relationship. He knew that his cause was just, and we assume that he possessed the force of character necessary to inspire others to follow him with confidence. The fact that he did not give way before the Amalekites during the long day of fighting implies that he had an infectious optimism that enabled him to inspire his men to persevere in the face of seemingly insurmountable odds.

Joshua must also have been a good judge of character, and he picked his men wisely (Exodus 17:9). He must also have been able to come up with a workable plan of action that enabled him to finally dominate the problems that faced him.[10]

Special Emphases

In conclusion, in our reading of this remarkable story, we do well to take note of certain themes that are repeated throughout the book. These include the fact that God was giving the Israelites the land of Canaan in keeping with His promise to Abraham, Isaac, and Jacob; that they were to go in and possess the land; that victory was assured; that the Lord would not fail or forsake them; and that God's people were to obey the Word that He had given through Moses.

We will see these emphases enlarged upon as we proceed with our study.

---

10. I have profited greatly from B. L. Montgomery's book *The Path to Leadership* (London: Collins, 1961), 256pp.

CHAPTER 1

THE GIFT OF THE LAND

JOSHUA 1:1-9

Moses, the great emancipator of God's people had brought the Israelites through the desert, and now all twelve tribes were camping on the wide, rich plain of Moab. The countryside was carpeted with wild flowers that provided a kaleidoscope of color. The land itself was watered by many small streams, and here and there grew stands of acacia trees where birds of the brightest plumage nested and raised their young. And farther south the scented oleanders added to what was already an idyllic setting. With such beauty all around them we are not surprised that the tribes of Reuben, Gad and half the tribe of Manasseh wished to stay on the eastern side of the River Jordan.

Moving westward, the grassland ended at the River Jordan, and a few short miles farther on was the city of Jericho, standing as a guardian over the road that led to the interior of Canaan.

It was in this setting that Moses gave his farewell address to the people and announced to them that he was soon to die. Fear must have gripped every heart, for who could possibly take the place of the one who had been a "father" to them for so many years. Then, after he had pronounced a special blessing on each tribe, the Israelites watched as he climbed to the top of Mount Nebo. None were permitted to follow him. From this summit the Lord showed him the land of Canaan in its length and breadth, and after that Moses breathed his last (Deuteronomy 34:5-7). So great was the loss felt by the Israelites that they mourned for him for an entire month. His "epitaph" in the Book of Deuteronomy was written either by the godly Eleazar or by his brave and noble son Phineas (Deuteronomy 34:10-12).

We noted in the Introduction to the Book of Joshua the fourfold division of the book. The Israelites were poised and ready to enter the Promised Land.

ENTERING THE LAND OF CANAAN, 1:1–5:15

The Commission of Joshua, 1:1-9

Who could possibly take Moses' place? The greatest men have no real successors.[1] Every truly good and noble and mighty man leaves behind him a vacuum that no other individual can fill. Take for example Samuel the prophet, or the psalmist David, or John the Baptist, or the Apostle Paul. Others continued the work that they had begun, but none could rival them in moral authority or accomplishment. And the same may be said of Alexander the Great, Julius Caesar, John Wycliffe, Martin Luther, and John Calvin. Each of these men stood related to the age in which he lived, and when he died his work had to be assigned to several individuals of lesser ability. And so, when we speak of

---

1. D. J. McCarthy, writing in *Biblica,* 52 (1971) 165-75, has attempted a possible "leadership theology."

Joshua as the *successor* of Moses, we use the term in a very limited sense.[2]

Transition in Leadership, 1:1-2a. "And it came to pass after the death of Moses the servant of Yahweh, that Yahweh spoke to Joshua the son of Nun, Moses' minister, saying, 'Moses my servant is dead.'"

There are a couple of very significant truths in this opening statement. First, the use of *"And"* implies a continuation of the sacred narrative. Though readers might be inclined to think of this historical survey as less important than the Torah written by Moses, the use of "and" places this work in the mainstream of God's inspired revelation.

Second, Moses is referred to as God's "servant." People assign titles to each other to designate their rank and importance (e.g., admiral or general, president or CEO, professor or doctor, bishop or pastor). However, the greatest title of all is to be called a "servant of God," and it is used of Moses over and over again–even when he is mentioned in the New Testament (Hebrews 3:5; cf. Revelation 15:3)! There is dignity as well as responsibility in being "a servant of God."

The Gift of the Land, 1:2b-4. Following the death of Moses, the Lord spoke personally to Joshua.[3] His command was clear: "Arise! Cross!" His imperatives are generally translated, "Now therefore arise, go over this Jordan, you,

---

2. Cf. T. Smith, *The History of Joshua*, 2d. ed. (Edinburgh: W. Oliphant, 1870), 18-19.

and all this people, into the land which I give to them, even to the children of Israel. Every place that the sole of your foot shall tread upon, to you have I have given it, as I spoke to Moses."[4]

We are not told where Joshua was when the Lord spoke to him, nor how God revealed His will. We do know that just before the death of Moses the Lord spoke to Moses and Joshua at the tent of meeting (Deuteronomy 31:14), and it is likely that God's word to Joshua on this occasion was communicated at the same place and in the same way. Of course, God's commission did not come as a surprise, for Joshua had been specifically designated to this office (Deuteronomy 1:38; 31:3, 6-8). But Joshua was now about ninety-three years of age, and it would have been natural for him to shrink from so great a responsibility.

The Promise of the Lord, 1:5-9. To encourage Joshua the Lord gave him a significant promise (Deuteronomy 11:24), and the extent of the land the Israelites were to possess was clearly spelled out.[5]

---

3. The frequency of God's "speaking" to the people of Israel or its leaders often depended on the nation's moral and spiritual condition.
4. "Your foot" suddenly has a plural pronoun suffix, though the verb is singular.
5. I have consistently used *The Macmillan Bible Atlas*, 3d ed., by Y. Aharoni and M. Avi-Yonah, revised by A. F. Rainey and A. Safrai (New York: Macmillan, 1993), even though the dating of events follows the liberal trend in biblical scholarship.

For a discussion of the Hittites, see O. R. Gurney, *The Hittites*, rev. ed. (London: Folio, 1990), 56-60; and H. A. Hoffner's essay in D. J. Wiseman's *Peoples of Old Testament Times* (Oxford: Clarendon, 1973), 197-228. The Lord's words "I have given it" (a future perfect tense of the verb) look upon the conquest of the land as if it were an accomplished fact. What is significant is the reference to "every place that the sole of your foot shall tread upon." God had given them the land, but they had to go in and possess it[6].

To reassure Joshua, the Lord made him a very specific promise: "There shall not any man be able to stand before you all the days of thy life; as I was with Moses, so I will be with you; I will not fail you, nor forsake you. Be strong and of good courage; for you shall cause this people to inherit the land which I swore to their fathers to give them. Only be strong and very courageous, to observe to do according to all the law, which Moses my servant commanded you: do not turn from it to the right hand or to the left, that you may have good success whithersoever you go."

Joshua had no illusions about the difficulties he faced. As one of the spies who had explored the land forty years earlier, he knew of the power of the Canaanites and of their formidable fortifications. That is why the Lord assured him of success. No one would be able to stand against him. But Joshua also knew of the difficulties involved in leading a

---

6. It is an important fact that at no time in the history of God's people did they possess all that God gave them, and so the full extent of God's gift awaits fulfillment in the future.

vast army. That is why the Lord encouraged him with the need to "be strong." The Lord also promised him victory over his adversaries. Joshua's sufficiency, however, was not of himself. The Lord would be with him and grant him good success.

The Lord then renewed Joshua's commission, "For you shall cause this people to inherit the land which I swore to their fathers to give them. Only be strong and very courageous, to observe to do according to all the Law, which Moses my servant commanded you: do not turn from it to the right hand or to the left, that you may have good success wherever you go. This book of the law shall not depart out of thy mouth, but you shall *meditate* therein day and night, that you may observe to do according to all that is written therein: for then you shall make your way prosperous, and then you shall have good success. Have not I commanded you? Be strong and of good courage; do not be afraid, neither be dismayed: for Yahweh your God is with you wherever you go" (1:6-9, emphasis added).

There are many scholarly men who believe that the books of Moses were written at a much later period (with Deuteronomy being penned around 622 during the reign of Josiah). This would make God's words to Joshua ludicrous, for how could he meditate on the Scriptures if none had been written? The fact that the Lord Himself refers to Moses' writings as extant at the time of Joshua should cause these learned theologians to rethink their position.

Let us note further that as important as it was for God's people to possess the scrolls written by Moses (cf. Romans

3:1-2), Joshua was to know from personal study and reflection what the Lord had communicated so that he could observe and do all that the Lord had commanded. It is possible that during the thirty-eight years of relative inactivity in the desert Joshua transcribed these documents so that he could have his own personal copy of all that Moses had written. We should also note that he was instructed to meditate on these Scriptures day and night (1:8). This would reinforce in his thinking what God had chosen to reveal.

Meditation has as its goal the application of truth to life. What Joshua was instructed to do is vastly different from the practice of those who seldom if ever open the Bible and believe that if they pay passing attention to a sermon on Sunday they have fulfilled their Christian duty.

We should also observe that God's command to Joshua concluded with the need for him to obey the Word. He was not given the option of picking and choosing the passages that he liked, for he was not to turn from what God had chosen to reveal to the right or the left. In other words, as the Apostle Paul later explained, all of God's Word is profitable for teaching, correction, and instruction in righteousness, so that the man of God may be completely furnished to perform every good work (2 Timothy 3:16,17).

Finally, there was God's definite assurance. By following the teaching of Scripture, and applying its teaching to his life, Joshua would enjoy good success.[7]

---

7. *Hiskil* "to have success," also conveys the idea (depending on the context) of "being prudent" or "acting in a circumspect way."

We often pay lip service to the Bible, but too few of us realize how vital is the counsel God has given us. The Bible is not like any other book. In a work entitled *Renewing Your Mind in a Secular World*[8] the editor included a chapter dealing with some research done to determine the individual mental and emotional health of people. The results of these tests showed that people could be divided into three categories:

- In *Group A* were those of superior mental and emotional health who possessed a high level of personal maturity.
- In *Group B* were those of average mental and emotional health, and a moderate level of maturity.
- In *Group C* were grouped those with below average mental and emotional health, and a significant level of psychological pain.

What is significant is the fact that in a longitudinal study those in *Group C* could move up to *Group B* by meditating on some passage of Scripture for about 20 minutes each day (Hebrews 4:12). The process would take about three years. And this change in mental and emotional health could be achieved without having to resort to psychologists and psychiatrists! Furthermore, those in *Group B,* with only average mental and emotional health, could move up to *Group A* and enjoy an enhanced sense of well-being by meditating on a passage of Scripture for about 20 minutes a day for three years.[9]

---

8. *Renewing Your Mind in a Secular World*, ed. J. D. Woodbridge (Chicago: Moody, 1985), 25-35.

The Bible is dynamic. It has the power to change the lives of those who diligently follow its teaching. What God said to Joshua is true. By meditating on successive portions of Scripture "day and night" the believer can "do wisely" and conduct himself/herself "appropriately" (i.e., with prudence and discretion) in the midst of a crooked and perverse generation, among whom he or she shines as a light in the world, holding fast the word of life (Philippians 2:15-16).

And this will result over time in the enjoyment of good success.

The Command to the People, 1:10-18

It has been observed that you can judge a leader by the size of the problems he tackles. In this section we will have occasion to observe the size of the task Joshua undertook.

Instructions Given to All Israel, 1:10-11. The Lord had spoken to Joshua, and now Joshua spoke to the people. They were to prepare for the invasion of the land that had been promised to their forefathers. The River Jordan, however, was in flood and this posed a significant barrier to anyone wanting to enter Canaan. And the fortifications of Jericho seemed impregnable! Imagine, therefore, the

---

9. This is not to ignore the value of the work of psychologists and psychiatrists. Their help should be sought where physiological issues (including abuse) have caused a variety of mental and/or emotional problems, and where antisocial behavior or psychopathic disorders make such intervention mandatory. In general, however, it should be borne in mind that change takes place through the renewing of the mind!

response of the people to the command of Joshua to prepare food for the invasion. Note his words to the officers: "Pass through the midst of the camp, and command the people, saying, 'Prepare food; for within three days you are to pass over this Jordan, to go in to possess the land which even now Yahweh your God is giving you to possess it.'"

What optimism! Joshua's words did more than focus the people's attention on the provisions that each family needed to set aside, his words also implied that victory was assured. Possession of the land, however, would not be brought about by their own strength or ingenuity. God would give them the land, and to Him alone should go their praise.

Instructions Given to the Transjordanian Tribes, 1:12-18. Next Joshua spoke with the tribes of Reuben, Gad, and half the tribe of Manasseh. Moses had given them an inheritance in the land of the Amorites (referred to as the "land toward the sunrise") whom they had defeated in battle (Numbers 21:25-35), on the condition that they help the other tribes take possession of Canaan when their brethren entered the land (Numbers 32:20-22). Now Joshua reminded them of their promise. Their wives, their little ones, and their cattle, would remain east of the River Jordan, but they should pass over before their brethren and help them conquer the land of Canaan. Once the land had been subdued, they could return to their inheritance (cf. 1:14-15).

The idea of "rest" looms large in Scripture. The whole concept is fascinating. God Himself is said to have rested on the seventh day from all His work (Genesis 2:2-3). Since

He is omnipotent, this "rest" was not necessitated by fatigue. His "rest" would seem to imply the satisfaction He experienced after having completed His work of creation. The word "rest" is also used in Scripture of death (Genesis 47:30; Deuteronomy 31:16), and of the peace individuals experience when they rest from their own work and trust implicitly in the work of Christ on their behalf (Matthew 11:28-29).

In the Book of Joshua "rest" speaks of peace and freedom from fear or warfare (cf. Deuteronomy 12:10; 25:19; Joshua 11:23).

In response to Joshua's words to the two-and-a-half tribes reminding them of what had taken place in the past, they responded: "All that you have commanded us we will do, and wherever you send us we will go. According as we hearkened unto Moses in all things, so will we hearken to you; only may Yahweh your God be with you, as he was with Moses. Whosoever rebels against your command, and does not hearken to your words in all that you command him, he shall be put to death: only be strong and of good courage" (1:16-18).

Far from needing to be coerced into fulfilling their earlier promise, these Israelites expressed their willingness to obey Joshua's every command. And so ardent were they in proclaiming their loyalty that they stood ready to deal in the most decisive way with anyone who might rebel against any command Joshua might issue.

But what does all of this have to do with us? It is appropriate at the end of each study to ask ourselves "So

What? What difference does this make?" In answering this question we are led to think specifically of God's Promises; God's Presence, and God's Word.

God's Promises

One of the first truths to impress itself on our minds is the importance to us of God's promises. His promises cover every aspect of our lives: e.g., wisdom to regulate our conduct (James 3:17-18), comfort and encouragement when we are downcast (Psalms 42:5, 11; 46:1), and assurance when we pass through the valley of the shadow (Psalm 23)--to name only a few. The Apostle Peter wrote: "Grace and peace be multiplied to you in the knowledge of God and of Jesus our Lord; seeing that His divine power has granted to us everything pertaining to life and godliness, through the true knowledge of Him who called us by His own glory and excellence. For by these He has granted to us His precious and magnificent promises, so that by them you may become partakers of the divine nature, having escaped the corruption that is in the world by lust" (2 Peter 1:2-4).

God's Presence

The Lord made Joshua a special promise. He said, "As I was with Moses, so I will be with you. I will not fail you, nor forsake you." This reminds us of the promise He has made to us. In Hebrews 13:5b-6 we read, "For He Himself has said, I will in no wise fail you, neither will I in any wise forsake you. So that with good courage we say, 'The Lord is my helper, I will not be afraid. What can man do to me?'" In the Greek text there are five negatives to assert as powerfully as language can that "the Lord will never, no never, no never depart" from us.

This promise results in a life of freedom without fear.

God's Word

Only as we invest time in pondering the truths of Scripture can the Word transform our lives, for it is through the renewing of our minds that we come progressively to approve the good and acceptable and perfect will of God (Romans 12:2). This truth is stated over and over in Scripture (cf. Colossians 2:6-7) using different figures of speech (e.g., Hebrews 5:13-14). Each, however, underscores the importance of meditating upon God's Word so that we become rooted and grounded in the truth, and through the use we make of Scripture are able to discern good and evil.

CHAPTER 2

THE MISSION OF THE SPIES

JOSHUA 2:1-24

The bicentennial celebration of the Lewis and Clark expedition prompted my wife and me to take a trip by paddlewheel steamship up the Columbia, Willamette, and Snake Rivers and retrace in part the epochal journey of these intrepid explorers. We spent our time sitting in lectures before visiting the places made famous by these bold and audacious pioneers.

One day we stopped for lunch at a restaurant conveniently situated on the bank of the river. A revolving book stand stood by the door leading into the gift shop, and as we entered I noticed a book entitled *Soiled Doves: Prostitution in the Early West* by Anne Seagraves.[1] Knowing that I would be writing on Rahab in this work on Joshua (and having no knowledge of prostitution apart from an occasional article in a Christian magazine), I decided to buy the book. Accordingly, after lunch, I made my way downstairs to the gift shop where I purchased the book.

---

1. A. Seagraves, *Soiled Doves* (Hayden, ID: Wesanne Publications, 1994), 175pp.

Ms. Seagraves' material is anything but salacious! It does reveal the dead-end lifestyle of those who through force of circumstance followed this profession. And no matter how hard one may try to gloss over the sordid lifestyle of the women who fell into this trap, the fact remains that they invariably led unfulfilled lives. One woman identified only as Madeleine said, "I could not make a demonstration of affection over men nor any pretense at response to their caresses. For the life of me I could not understand why they should expect it. They had only bought my body. I could not see why they should want more. My love was not for sale, piecemeal, to everyman who had the price to pay for my body."

All too often those who first served in a "house of pleasure" succumbed to alcohol and drugs and eventually ended their dreary lives in the gutter feeling *worthless* (i.e., rejected by men because their beauty had faded and their clients preferred younger, prettier women), *used*, and *sick* in both body and soul.

Life for these "soiled doves" was hard and the only hope any of them had of a brighter future lay in opening their own "establishment." As a "madam" they naturally took a portion of the earnings of each of "their girls" so that in time, and with diligent saving, they could obtain a legitimate business. But few women of easy virtue succeeded in breaking away from the entrapment of their profession.

God was gracious to Rahab. It would seem as if she had realized the shortcomings of her profession and so had developed a sideline working with flax. As her story unfolds she gives testimony to her faith in Israel's God and her belief in His sovereignty. She speaks assuredly of her confidence in His power (2:10), majesty (2:11), and mercy (2:12-13).

We might have expected her to pass from the pages of Scripture with scarcely any additional reference, but later New Testament writers do not hesitate to mention her as an example of remarkable faith (cf. Hebrews 11:31; James 2:25).

Earlier in our study we considered God's appointment of a new leader. With the death of Moses the Israelites spent a full month mourning his passing. This period of grieving was important. It served as a transition between the one era that had come to an end and a new one that was about to begin. As this period of national lamentation neared its end Joshua called to him two men whom he could trust. To them he gave a specific assignment: They were to leave the place where they had set up their tents, make their way to the River Jordan (a distance of about seven miles), swim the river that was then at flood stage, and spy out the land.[2] As the new commander, Joshua did not want to repeat the problems of Kadesh-Barnea (Numbers 13:1–14:45) and so he hand-picked the men and sent them away secretly (2:1a).[3]

---

2. The spies were sent out and returned before the order of 1:10 was given.

The Mission of the Spies, 2:1-24

The city of Jericho was plainly visible from the eastern bank of the River Jordan, for it occupied a prominent position on a hill and guarded the road leading to the interior of Canaan. The men probably swam the river carrying their clothes in watertight skin bags. Once in Canaan they quickly changed and then linked up with the road (called "The Way to the Jordan") that ran from Jericho to the River Jordan. In this way they hoped they could approach Jericho without attracting undue attention.

Jericho is referred to in Scripture as "the city of palm trees," and the spies must have been struck by the extraordinary beauty and luxuriant vegetation of the district, for they passed ripened wheat fields, fig trees laden with fruit, and a variety of other shrubs all irrigated by the streams that flowed through the valley. Early travelers to the area have spoken eloquently of the flora and fauna, and claim that every tree is tenanted by the Palestinian nightingale, the hopping thrush, the gorgeous Indian kingfisher, the Egyptian turtle-dove, and other birds of Indian and Abyssinian affinity.[4]

---

3. Now, Joshua the son of Nun had sent out of Shittim two men as spies secretly, saying, "Go, view the land, and Jericho" (2:1a). The words *vu-yishlah*, "had sent," imply that what is recorded in this chapter occurred before 1:10 when Joshua issued instructions for the Israelites to prepare for the invasion of Canaan.
4. Cf. H. B. Tristram, *The Land of Israel* (London: SPCK, 1865), 203ff.

Dr. Edward Robinson, who visited the Holy Land and wrote of all that he saw, claims that "the climate of Jericho is excessively hot.... According to our Arabs, the sojourn of a single night is often sufficient to occasion a fever. Nor is this surprising, when we consider, that the cauldron of the Dead Sea and the valley of the Jordan lie thirteen hundred feet below the level of the ocean."[5] Obviously the Israelites had been conditioned to heat as a result of their desert experience, and those living in the area must have become accustomed to the climatic conditions of the Jordan valley.

The Woman Whose Heart God Had Opened, 2:1b. After walking along the twelve miles that led along the main road leading to Jericho the spies made their way to the house of "a woman, a harlot" named Rahab. And they rested there as they waited for a suitable time to speak with her.

Great pains have been taken by those embarrassed at the thought that a whore could be an ancestor of the Lord Jesus (Matthew 1:5) that they have tried to clear Rahab's character of all odious connotations by claiming that she was a "hostess" or innkeeper, and not a prostitute. References in the New Testament, however, clearly identify her as a harlot (cf. Hebrews 11:31; James 2:25), though she may also have provided meals for those wayfarers who came to her home. Dr. George Bush, who taught at the State University of New York, places Rahab's actions in a more accurate light: "It is to be remembered, that Rahab lived in the

---

5. E. Robinson, *Biblical Researches in Palestine*, 3 vols. (London: Murray, 1856), I:553.

midst of a people, corrupt, abandoned, and profligate to the last degree. Vices of the most enormous and debasing character were practiced without reserve, and received the sanction of every class of people."[6] In short, Rahab was a product of her culture and did not carry the opprobrium that a strumpet does today.

The spies have also been roundly criticized for going to a place of ill-repute, even though there is no evidence that they availed themselves of Rahab's services. In actual fact, the spies chose the best possible place to obtain information. Where else could they find anyone so well-informed? Rahab was in a unique position to know of political and economic trends taking place in the countries bordering on Canaan. She had heard from travelers coming from Egypt of the way in which the God of the Israelites had parted the waters of the Red Sea, and though this had happened forty years earlier (and its impact on the surrounding nations had in all probability lessened with the passing of time) yet she had taken the story to heart and believed what had been told her. She had also entertained Amorites from across the River Jordan and learned from them how the Israelites had conquered the powerful armies of Sihon and Og (2:10). Her heart had melted with fear as she thought of the power of One so great that He could roll back the waters of the Red Sea, and bring to their knees Sihon and Og--two of the mightiest monarchs of her day.

---

6. G. Bush, *Notes on the Book of Joshua* (Minneapolis: Klock and Klock, 1981), 31.

The King Who Trembled on His Throne, 2:2-6. "And it was told the king of Jericho, saying, 'Behold, men came here tonight[7] of the children of Israel to search out the land.' And the king of Jericho sent to Rahab, saying, 'Bring forth the men that are come to you, that have entered into your house; for they have come to search out all the land.'"

It may have seemed as if Rahab had just learned of the mission of the spies when she heard a commotion in the street and surmised that messengers from the king had come to take into custody her visitors. Acting quickly, she took the men to the roof of her house and "hid him"[8] beneath flax that she was drying on the roof.[9]

The soldiers from the king knew that hospitality was a sacred duty throughout the ancient Near East, and so did not barge in and search Rahab's home. Believing that she may have been "occupied" they waited respectfully for her to

---

7. There is a high ridge or mountain to the west of Jericho that casts a shadow over Jericho by mid-afternoon. This may explain the reference to "shutting the gate at dark" (2:5).
8. The Hebrew has the singular (implying that she may have hidden each man separately in a different part of the roof).
9. S. Talmon, *Journal of the American Oriental Society*, 83 (1963), 177-87. In addition to Rahab's involvement in prostitution, she was also an industrious person involved in a legitimate occupation like the virtuous woman in Proverbs 31:13. She was also concerned for the lives of the two men who had fortuitously come to her home. This is a far cry from the calloused, uncaring attitude of others in her profession who are generally only interested in making money.

come to the door of her house. When she appeared they told her of the danger posed by these men, and asked Rahab to bring them out.

Rahab's response was: "Yes, the men came to me, but I did not know where they were from." She let the king's messenger's believe that the Israelites were just two patrons from whom it was not customary to ask for credentials. Then she continued, "And it came to pass about the time of the shutting of the gate, when it was dark, that the men went out; whither the men went, I know not: pursue after them quickly; for you will overtake them" (2:4b-5).

Rahab's lie to the king's soldiers has caused those who try to excuse her conduct to have conniptions. How can she be held up as an example of faith and yet be guilty of such unashamed deception? Then, to try and avoid others using her as an excuse for prevarication, they remind us that God desires truth in our inward part (Leviticus 19:11; Psalm 51:6; Proverbs 12:22; Ephesians 4:25), and that no lie is ever justifiable.[10] That Rahab deceived the king's messengers is unquestioned, but is that all? Accurate interpretation must be based on the critical, historical and cultural method of hermeneutics. It behooves us to remember that Rahab had been reared among the depraved Canaanites, and had probably never been taught the evil of lying.

Lying has been, and still is, a universal practice among people of the Middle East. In our recent history we need

---

10. This view is espoused by H. C. Trumbull, *A Lie Never Justifiable* (Philadelphia: J. D. Wattles, 1893), 237pp.

only think of the lies told by Saddam Hussein and his Iraqi associates, and the deceptive strategies of the Iranians in covering up their efforts to produce nuclear bombs. We should not be surprised, therefore, that Rahab resorted to such a practice. Furthermore, in war it is often necessary for people behind enemy lines to mislead those who would do them harm. In exercising her newly found faith, Rahab identified herself with the people of Israel, and their enemies became her enemies.

With verse 6 the biblical historian provides us with a flashback. The roofs of houses were flat, and among the Hebrews were furnished with a parapet (Deuteronomy 22:8). In hot weather people could sleep on the roof where the evening breeze would afford them some relief from the oppressive heat. Rahab was drying flax on the roof prior to beating it and preparing it for spinning. And this was where she hid the spies.

The Profitless Search, 2:7. In misleading the king's messengers Rahab said, "The men [whom you seek] came unto me ... but when it was dark the men went out; whither the men went I know not: pursue after them quickly; for you will overtake them.... And the men pursued after them the way to the Jordan: and as soon as they that pursued after them were gone out, they shut the gate."

The shutting of the gate adds a humorous touch to the story. Just in case the Israelites had not left the city, the people of Jericho wanted to make sure they did not escape.

The Woman's Bold Confession of Faith, 2:8-13. Rahab then returned to the spies on the roof of her house.

There she spoke of her belief: "I know that Yahweh has given you the land, and that the fear of you has fallen upon us, and that all the inhabitants of the land melt away before you. For we have heard how Yahweh dried up the water of the Red Sea before you, when you came out of Egypt; and what you did to the two kings of the Amorites that were beyond the Jordan, to Sihon and to Og, whom you utterly destroyed. And as soon as we had heard it, our hearts did melt, neither did there remain any more spirit in any man [lit., no man's spirit was erect within him], because of you: for Yahweh your God, He is God in heaven above, and on earth beneath. Now therefore, I pray you, swear unto me by Yahweh, since I have dealt kindly with you, that you also will deal kindly with my father's house, and give me a true token; and that you will save alive my father, and my mother, and my brothers, and my sisters, and all that they have, and will deliver our lives from death."

It is easy to read these words without sensing the emotion that prompted them. Here is Rahab's emphatic declaration of her faith in the one, true God. It is more than a shrewd conjecture based upon the information shared with her by travelers. What she had learned awakened in her a realization of the fact that Israel's God was omnipotent and omnipresent. And having come to this belief, we are not surprised that she turned away from the false gods and idolatrous worship of her countrymen.

It is also interesting to note that the people of Jericho had heard the same reports, but they were not moved to take action. The Lord graciously responded to Rahab and set in motion a plan that would spare her and her family from the destruction that was soon to overtake the city.

Furthermore, we catch a note of the woman's earnestness in verse 12 when she says, *"Now therefore, I pray you, swear unto me by Yahweh ...."* Dr. George Bush's comments upon this verse are most apropos: "[Her] proposal still further displays the sincerity and strength of her faith. While the people of Israel, with the miracles of the Divine power constantly before their eyes, were incessantly prone to stagger at the promises and give way to unbelief, she upon a hearsay report of these wonders, is so firmly persuaded of their truth, that she desires to enter into a covenant with the spies for her own preservation and that of her family. In like manner, a deep-rooted conviction of the danger hanging over the head of the sinner from the curse of a violated law, will prompt him to give all diligence to flee from the wrath to come and lay hold of eternal life by joining himself to God and His people."[11]

Rahab asked for some word of confirmation that she and her family would be saved alive. There is no mention of a husband, and from this we infer that she either was a widow or had never been married. The latter is more likely, for had she been married it would have been abhorrent for her to maintain a brothel with her husband in the home.

The Promise of the Spies, 2:14-21a. To her earnest request the spies responded: "Our life for yours, if you do not utter this our business; and it shall be, when Yahweh

---

11. Bush, *Joshua*, 37-38.

gives us the land, that we will deal kindly and truly with you." Then she let them down[12] by a cord through the window: for her house was upon the side of the wall, and she dwelt upon the wall. And she said to them, "Go to the mountain, lest the pursuers find on you; and hide yourselves there three days, until the pursuers have returned: and afterward may you go your way."

And the men said unto her, "We will be guiltless of this your oath which you have made us swear, unless when we come into the land, you do not bind this line of scarlet thread in the window by which you have let us down: and you shall gather to you into the house your father, and your mother, and your brothers, and all your father's household. And it shall be, that whosoever shall go out of the doors of your house into the street, his blood shall be upon his head, and we shall be guiltless: and whosoever shall be with you in the house, his blood shall be on our head, if any hand be upon him. But if you utter this our business, then we shall be guiltless of your oath which you have made us swear." And she said, "According to your words, so be it."

The plural of "you" (2:14) includes any change of heart that she may have or any attempt on the part of a member of her father's house to betray them to the king or any of his officials.

---

12. *Wattoridem*, "had lowered," is one of the many past perfects in this book. This storytelling device has been discussed by W. J. Martin, *Vetus Testamentum Supplement* 17 (1969), 182.

The Escape of the Spies, 2:21b-22. Rahab's parting words to the spies urge them to flee westward to "the mountain," while those soldiers who sought to capture them had gone eastward along the road that eventually led to the River Jordan. With the terms of the agreement clearly understood the spies vanished into the darkness. There are numerous caves in this mountain range, and the spies could hide in any number of them without being detected.[13] They stayed in the mountain until the pursuers had returned, and then made their way back to the camp of Israel.

The requirement of the spies that a scarlet cord be tied in the window to mark Rahab's house has been thought by some Bible scholars to form the same function as the blood sprinkled on the door posts and lintel of the homes of the Hebrews in Egypt when the Angel of the Lord went through the land and killed all the firstborn. Though there are many fine preachers who believe that the scarlet cord did fulfill this purpose, there is no direct parallel between the events.

---

13. The late Dr. Joseph Free, for many years professor of Archaeology, Wheaton College, IL, in his *Archaeology and Bible History* (Wheaton, IL: Scripture Press, 1962), 127-28, describes the scene for us: "When Rahab let the spies down from her house on the wall, she directed them to go to 'the mountain' to hide until their pursuers would return from their search.... Jericho lies in the plain of the Jordan, which at this point is about fourteen miles wide .... Jericho is near the western end of the valley. As one looks north, south, and east no nearby mountain meets the eye ... but just about a mile to the west lies the edge of the rugged plateau ridge which is the beginning of the hills forming the Judean wilderness."

The Report of the Spies, 2:23-24. After three days the spies returned to Joshua. Once before him they told him all that had happened. In particular they mentioned how the Canaanites had become dispirited and were fearful of the coming invasion.

As we review the contents of this chapter it is appropriate for us to see that faith and works are intertwined. They go together, and in the case of Rahab are closely connected with courage and the need to take God seriously. It is clear from Rahab's confession of faith that she had come to believe in an infinite, personal God who is transcendent as well as immanent, who created the universe, sustains it by His power, and who acts in supernatural ways (2:10-11).

What is illustrated so plainly in the example of Rahab has caused some philosophical theologians (and their followers) to spend endless hours wrangling over the supposed dichotomy between faith and works. Rahab had heard of God's mighty deeds from travelers who had come to her door. Those who came from Egypt would gather about them a group of eager listeners just by saying, "Have you heard what the Hebrew God did in Egypt?" And then there would be a rehearsal of the plagues, the parting of the Red Sea, and the destruction of Pharaoh's army.

On other occasions people from east of the River Jordan would tell how the ragged rabble from the desert (viz., the Israelites) had defeated the well-disciplined armies of Sihon and Og, and taken over their land. And some who had witnessed Balak's summons of Balaam to curse the Israelites, would recount how the prophet from the Euphrates had blessed God's people instead of cursing them, and how, in his prophetic forecast, Balaam had promised Israel victory over all its enemies.

As Rahab had listened to these reports, the Holy Spirit had opened her heart (John 16:8). The more she heard the stronger grew her faith. The writer of Hebrews captured all this when he wrote: "*By faith* Rahab the harlot did not perish along with those who were disobedient, after she had welcomed the spies in peace" (Hebrews 11:31, emphasis added). And James, our Lord's brother, emphasized the need for works to give proof of genuine faith when he wrote: "In like manner was not also Rahab the harlot justified by works, in that she received the messengers, and sent them out another way?" (James 2:25). Her faith was so strong that she risked her life in order to protect the spies. God honored her faith, and when Jericho was attacked Rahab and her family were spared.

The grace of God is also evident in the sequel to this story of Rahab. Once secure within the protection of the people of Israel, Rahab married a Hebrew named Salmon (whom many believe was one of the spies). In time the Lord honored her by allowing her to conceive and bear a son. And through her son she became an ancestor of King David and ultimately of the Lord Jesus Himself (Matthew 1:5).

All of this gives evidence of the grace of God and the need to take Him and His Word seriously. There are many today who are wilfully ignorant of the teaching of Scripture. They may hold fast to certain verses that support their political or sociological position, but they are happy to measure themselves by themselves and compare themselves with themselves (cf. 2 Corinthians 10:12). Such wilful ignorance of God's plan of salvation causes them to look at the surrounding walls of their secular city and conclude that they are perfectly safe. But they are not. They are as answerable to the Lord God as were the people of Jericho.

But where does this leave us? Rahab believed that God had a special plan for His people, and that they were to be His rod to punish her people for their sins.[14] Acting upon this belief she boldly identified herself with the Israelites. The rest of those in Jericho had the same opportunity to turn to the Lord, but they neglected to avail themselves of the brief period of grace that was offered them.

---

14. Many have argued that God was unjust in punishing the Canaanites and Amorites and giving their land to the Israelites. This position has been ably refuted by the late Dr. John Kitto in his valuable *Daily Bible Illustrations*, 2 vols. (Grand Rapids: Kregel, 1981), 478-80.

CHAPTER 3

THE CROSSING OF THE RIVER JORDAN

Part One

JOSHUA 3:1–4:24

In certain sections of the Christian church allegorism is a popular approach to the interpretation of the Old Testament. It is believed that this method makes the events of the Old Testament applicable to people living in modern times. When this procedure is applied to the early history of Israel, their bondage in Egypt is likened to fallen, helpless humanity sold under sin; the Exodus from Egypt is believed to portray the redemption of the believer by Christ; the wandering of the tribes in the desert is thought to depict the Christian's continuous unrest as he or she strives with the world, the flesh, and the devil; and the crossing of the River Jordan is believed to prefigure the believer's death with Canaan being symbolic of heaven.

Samuel Stennett (1727-1795) followed this line of interpretation. At one time his hymn entitled *On Jordan's Stormy Banks* was very popular. One stanza reads:

> On Jordan's stormy banks I stand
> and cast a wishful eye
> to Canaan's fair and happy land,

where my possessions lie.
All o'er those wide extended plains
shines one eternal day;
where God the Son forever reigns
and scatters night away....
When shall I reach that happy place
and be forever blest?
When shall I see my Father's face
and in His bosom rest?

As beautiful as this hymn is, this was not the expectation of the Israelites as they stood on the eastern bank of the River Jordan. Their inheritance in the land of Canaan would only be theirs as they defeated and dispossessed those living in the land and took possession of their cities and farms.

We continue our study of Israel's entrance into the Promised Land with "The Crossing of the River Jordan."

The Bridgehead, 3:1-17.

The River Jordan is a ravine within a ravine. Down the lower part runs the river. At the time of the Israelite encampment on the plains of Moab the River Jordan was in flood. Those in Jericho probably felt reasonably safe behind their city's double walls, for the river was deemed to be impassable at this time of year. The people in Jericho probably believed that only two courses lay open to the Israelites: (1) journey north and cross the Jordan below Lake Huleh, or (2) journey south and cross into Canaan by circling around the lower end of the Dead Sea. If they chose the former they would face a coalition of the northern kingdoms, and if they opted for the latter they would face a coalition of the southern kingdoms. God, however, chose neither route.

Joshua's Command to the People, 3:1-5. "And Joshua rose up early in the morning; and they removed from Abel-Shittim ['the meadow of the Acacias'], and came to the Jordan, he and all the children of Israel; and they lodged there before they passed over. And it came to pass after three days, that the officers went through the midst of the camp; and they commanded the people, saying, 'When you see the Ark of the Covenant of Yahweh your God, with the Levitical priests bearing it, then you shall remove from your place, and go after it. Yet there shall be a space between you and it, about two thousand cubits by measure: do not come near it, that you may know the way by which you must go; for you have not passed this way heretofore.'"

"And Joshua said to the people, 'Sanctify yourselves; for tomorrow Yahweh will do wonders among you.'"

Though the Israelite camp was only about seven miles from the bank of the River Jordan, moving all the people and their livestock was a mammoth undertaking. The people numbered about two million, and the difficulty of Joshua's task can best be understood when we consider what happened when Barak, king of Moab, hired Balaam to curse God's people. The Israelites were spread over such a vast area that at no time could Balaam see the entire camp (cf. Numbers 22:41b; 23:13; 24:2). Now all these people had to move across the flooded river.

Joshua's first command had to do with the Ark of the Covenant. It was to lead the way. During the wandering of God's people in the desert the tribes had been guided by the Shekinah Glory (manifested in the pillar of cloud by day and the pillar of fire by night. Cf. Numbers 9:21). Now, they were to be guided by the Ark of the Covenant. It had always signified the presence of God among His people. In the past the Kohathites had carried the Ark. Now it was to be carried by the Levitical priests. The people were to maintain a distance of 2,000 cubits (i.e., about 3,000 feet or 1,000 yards) so that they would know which way to go.

Joshua also commanded the people to "sanctify" themselves. Based on Exodus 19:10-14 this involved washing their persons and their clothes, and abstaining from everything that might take their minds off the seriousness of the task that lay before them.

Joshua's Command to the Priests, 3:6. "And Joshua spoke unto the priests, saying, 'Take up the Ark of the Covenant, and pass over before the people.' And they took up the Ark of the Covenant, and went before the people." According to Numbers 7:9 poles were to be inserted through rings in the sides of the Ark, so that it could be carried on the shoulders of those designated to bear it. And that is what happened on this occasion.

God's Encouragement to Joshua, 3:7-8. "Now Yahweh had said unto Joshua, 'This day I will begin to magnify you in the sight of all Israel, that they may know that, as I was with Moses, so I will be with you. And you shall command the priests that bear the Ark of the Covenant, saying,

"When you come to the brink of the waters of the [River] Jordan, you shall stand still in the Jordan.'"

God planned to do a work as significant as the parting of the waters of the Red Sea (cf. 4:23-24), and this would enhance Joshua in the eyes of the people. His power would also confirm the fact that Joshua was not alone in leading the people against so formidable an enemy.[1]

Joshua's Charge to the Israelites, 3:9-13. "And Joshua said to the children of Israel, 'Come here, and hear the words of Yahweh your God.' And Joshua said, 'Hereby you shall know that the living God [El] is among you, and that he will without fail drive out from before you the Canaanite[2], and the Hittite, and the Hivite, and the Perizzite, and the Girgashite, and the Amorite[3], and the Jebusite. Behold, the Ark of the Covenant of the Lord of all the earth passes over before you into the Jordan. Now therefore take twelve men out of the tribes of Israel, for every tribe a man. And it shall come to pass, when the soles of the feet of the priests that bear the Ark of Yahweh shall rest in the waters of the Jordan, that the waters of the Jordan shall be cut off, even the waters that come down from above; and they shall stand in one heap.'"

---

1. Cf. The reaction of the Israelites when Moses received the report of the twelve spies (Numbers 13–14). The "giants" (men of great stature) were still in the land, and so were their well fortified cities.
2. See Wiseman, *Peoples of Old Testament Times*, 29-52.
3. Ibid., 100-133.

Joshua began with an invitation to all the Israelites to come within the sound of his voice. The Lord must have enabled what he said to carry over a great distance, for everyone heard him. He began by assuring them that "the *living* God" was among them. He was not a dull, senseless image like the gods of the heathen (cf. Psalm 115:3-8), but a living, intelligent, powerful Being whose abiding presence would give them the victory over all their enemies.

But there was still the River Jordan to be crossed, and to the Israelites it formed a formidable barrier.

Joshua assured the people that the Ark of the Covenant (symbolizing God's presence) would lead the way,[4] and as soon as the feet of the priests touched the waters of the Jordan the river would be cut off. Those waters coming down from above would rise up, and those going down to the Dead Sea would be drained off leaving several miles of river bed that could be safely crossed.

The Obedience of the People, 3:14-17. "And it came to pass, when the people removed from their tents, to pass over the Jordan, the priests that bore the Ark of the Covenant went before the people; and when they were come to the Jordan, and their feet were dipped in the brink of the water (for the Jordan overflowed at its banks all the time of harvest[5]), that the waters which came down from above stood, and rose up in one heap, a great way off, at Adam, the city that is beside Zarethan [about 18 miles north of where

---

4. According to Numbers 10:35-36 the Ark was synonymous with the "Lord" who was among them (cf. 2 Samuel 6:2).

the Israelites were]; and those that went down toward the sea of the Arabah, (namely the Dead Sea), were wholly cut off: and the people [with their sheep and cattle] passed over right in front of Jericho. And the priests that bore the Ark of the Covenant of Yahweh stood firm on dry ground in the middle of the Jordan; and all Israel passed over on dry ground, until all the nation had passed over the Jordan."

This is another example of faith and works going together. Everything happened exactly as the Lord had instructed Joshua. We could wish that the Church today was as quick to obey the commands of Christ. All too often our leaders reinterpret the text of Scripture to suit their own views on specific matters, and then wonder why the Lord has removed the church's lampstand from its place (Revelation 2:5). But how are we to explain the fact that the Jordan suddenly stopped flowing? The Bible clearly states that the river was in flood.

There are some negative students of the Bible who do *not* believe that the river was in flood.[6] Others believe that we have here the record of a natural occurrence. It is their contention that over time the river had undermined one of

---

5. The overflow occurs in the late winter to early spring, when the river is swollen initially by the long winter rains and later by the melting snows of the Anti-Lebanon mountain range.
6. Robinson, *Biblical Researches*, I:353-44, has an excellent description of the Jordan valley, but claims that he was not able to find any flooding of the river that would confirm the biblical account. Climatic changes and the lessening of snowfall on the Lebanon mountains might account for the Jordan swelling only to the top of the second rim.

its banks. This collapsed at a most fortuitous time, thus blocking off the flow of water at Adam (identified today with *ed- Damiyeh)*, and that this landslide blocked the flow of the River Jordan. Landslides have occurred in this region before.[7] As convenient as this view appears, there are problems associated with it. There is no indication that landslides blocked the other streams south of Adam that flow into the Jordan. Furthermore, even though the landslide could have occurred at precisely the time the priests carrying the Ark entered the Jordan, it cannot account for the miraculous drying up of the river so that the Israelites "crossed on dry ground."[8]

Israel's bridgehead into Canaan was effected directly opposite Jericho. And the people of Jericho, having relied on the river to form a barrier between them, must now have had their earlier apprehensions intensified.

---

7. The landslides of 1267, 1906, and 1927 temporarily stopped the flow of the River Jordan. However, Judges 5:4 and Psalm 114:3-4 imply that an earthquake occurred at the time the Israelites crossed the River Jordan. It is true that God can and does use means to accomplish His purposes. The text of Joshua makes explicit the fact that the parting of the waters of the River Jordan was a miracle, and the stretch of dried up river sufficiently long that several thousand people could cross at one time. Cf. J. Garstang, *Joshua/Judges* (Grand Rapids: Kregel, 1978), 136-37; and H.-J. Kraus, *Vetus Testamentum*, 1 (1951), 181-89.
8. Another explanation is advanced by J. N. M. Wijnhaards, *Oudetestamentische Studien*, 16 (1969), 1-132, in which she believes that the entire "from Shittim to Gilgal" story is fictitious and has been taken from a prior tradition.

What do we learn from this incident? There are many lessons of practical importance, but we shall concentrate only on what they reveal about God and His attributes. As we do so it is important for us to remember that an attribute is a property intrinsic to its subject, by which the subject is distinguished or identified.

The Person of God

The Israelites must have viewed the obstacles facing them with human feelings of apprehension. It was necessary, therefore, for Joshua to encourage them with the assurance that the *living God* was among them. In saying this he immediately contrasted Him with the idols worshiped by the heathen. The Lord had already protected them, kept them safe in battle, and enabled them to defeat kings and kingdoms more powerful than themselves.

As we reflect on what Scripture teaches we also note God's power and timing. The Bible portrays the Lord of heaven and earth as infinite, eternal, all-powerful, all-wise, and everywhere present. His names highlight who He is and emphasize His person and work.[9]

In this chapter He is referred to as *Yahweh* (printed "LORD" in most versions, and occasionally "Jehovah" in some older versions), signifying His self-existence. He had

---

9. "Imminent." This is an attribute of God meaning that He is close at hand and involved in the things that go on (a) in the world, and (b) in our lives. This teaching must be balanced with an understanding of God's "transcendence" (i.e., being above and beyond the world and unaffected by what takes place on earth).

no beginning and will have no end. He is the supreme ruler of the universe. He is also referred to as *'adon*, a shortened form of *'adonay*, meaning "Lord" or "Master," and emphasizing the fact that He is all-powerful and has the right to be obeyed. It also signifies that He is our supreme Sovereign who has the right to be worshiped. And other Scriptures that speak of Yahweh-Jireh, Yahweh-Nissi, Yahweh-Shammah, et cetera, when taken together, reveal the perfection of God's character and the extent of His work on our behalf. And in Joshua 3:3 and 10, He is referred to as *'Elohim* ("God"), signifying His power and might. No other god can compare with Him.

Scripture confirms that our God is the Lord of heaven and earth (Genesis 24:3). He is sovereign over the kingdoms of the earth, and as such He is also Judge (Psalms 50:6; 58:11). And He is the Savior of those who put their trust in Him (Isaiah 45:15).

God is so involved in human affairs that He can be known by, and answer the prayers of, those with whom He has established a covenant relationship. The great blessing of knowing "the living God" as He is revealed in Scripture is that He becomes the standard by which all things are to be measured. And He becomes the one after whom character is to be patterned (Leviticus 20:26). Those who are in a covenant relationship with Him should respond to lovingkindness with trust and obedience.

The Promises of God

Joshua was assured of God's personal promises: (1) He would be with him as He had been with Moses; (2) no one would be able to stand before him; and (3) to this the Lord added that He would magnify Joshua in the eyes of the people. All of this the Lord did.

Similar promises have been made to Christians. First, in the New Testament we are made aware of the truth that God the Holy Spirit indwells us, and we are assured of His presence wherever we go, no matter what may happen to us. We are also promised that He gives eternal salvation to all who believe in Christ (Hebrews 13:5, John 3:16). Second, though we are not promised unlimited secular success, the Holy Spirit does empower us and enable us to stand for what is right no matter how strong the opposition. And third, in 1 Corinthians 1:26-27 we learn that we have an adoption that has made us sons and daughters of God.

The more these truths take a hold of us, the greater will be our confidence when we face the vicissitudes of life.

CHAPTER 4

THE CROSSING OF THE RIVER JORDAN

Part Two

JOSHUA 3:1–4:24

The Memorial, 4:1-24

The way in which the Bible records the entrance of the Israelites into the Promised Land leaves us with the impression that it was accomplished with relative ease. Like complimentary bookends the text of Scripture reads: "Then Joshua rose early in the morning; and he and all the sons of Israel set out from Shittim and came to the Jordan, and they lodged there before they crossed" (3:1). This is followed by "and when all the nation had finished crossing the Jordan ..." (4:1 NASB). Little space is given to the logistics involved.

While camping on the plains of Moab the Israelites probably maintained their tribal positions around the Tabernacle. The tribes of Benjamin, (half the tribe of) Manasseh and Ephraim would have been on the west; Naphtali, Asher and Dan would have pitched their tents on the north; Judah, Issachar and Zebulun would have set up their tents on the east; and the tribes of Reuben, Simeon and Gad would be situated closest to the Dead Sea. When Joshua issued the order for them to move down to the River Jordan the people struck camp and moved westward, maintaining the marching positions adhered to throughout all their wilderness wandering. On the bank of the River Jordan they spread themselves out over several miles. Then, when the order came for them to follow the Ark and cross the river, they did so.

We are so accustomed to watching western movies, in which pioneer settlers with their covered wagons crossed rivers with relative ease, that we expect the Israelites to have done the same. In the movies these crossings were done at places where the approach to the river was fairly gradual and the water not too deep. Even then, some wagons were lost and some cattle were swept down stream. The situation facing the Israelites was entirely different. There was no gradual descent into the River Jordan. The people, with their belongings and their cattle, had to descend a bank to the fairly level ground that until recently had been covered with the Jordan's torrent. This fairly level plain had to be traversed before they could descend another steep bank to the river bed. Once crossed, they had to climb up both banks before they could stake out a place for themselves facing Jericho a short distance away.[1]

Of course, the activity of the Israelites was watched with growing apprehension by those inside Jericho.

Two Permanent Reminders, 4:1-9. "And it came to pass, when all the nation had finished crossing the Jordan, that Yahweh spoke to Joshua[2], saying, 'Take twelve men from among the people, one man from each tribe, and command them, saying, "Take up for yourselves twelve stones from the midst of the Jordan, from the place where the priests' feet are standing, and carry them over with you and lay them down in the lodging-place where you will lodge tonight." " "

"Then Joshua called the twelve men[3], whom he had appointed from the sons of Israel, one man from each tribe; and Joshua said unto them, 'Pass over before the Ark of Yahweh your God into the middle of the Jordan, and each of you take up a stone on his shoulder, according to the number of the tribes of the children of Israel. Let this be a sign among you, that, when your children ask in time to come, saying, "What do these stones mean?" then you shall say to them, "Because the waters of the Jordan were cut off before the Ark of the Covenant of Yahweh ...." So these stones shall be a memorial to the sons of Israel forever.'"

---

1. Included among those who crossed the dry river bed were 40,000 armed men from the tribes of Reuben, Gad and the half-tribe of Manasseh (4:12-13). This was less than 50 per cent of the total fighting force of these tribes. The remainder of the men stayed on the eastern side of the River Jordan to protect the lands and families of those who had chosen to receive their inheritance in the lands formerly occupied by the Amorites.
2. The importance of the divine initiative is stressed repeatedly by the inspired historian.
3. "Twelve" occurs five times in verses 1-8. It seems as if the writer was stressing the involvement of the whole nation, for one man came from each of the twelve tribes.

"And the sons of Israel did so as Joshua commanded, and took up twelve stones out of the midst of the Jordan, as Yahweh spake to Joshua ... and they carried them over with them unto the place where they lodged, and laid them down there" (4:1-8).

In reality, two memorials were set up, the one at Gilgal and the other in the River Jordan, for we read: "And Joshua set up twelve stones in the middle of the Jordan, at the place where the ... priests ... stood: and they are there unto this day." The *New International Version of the Bible* changes the text of verse 9 to make it the same as verse 5, even though two memorials are found in ancient versions like the Septuagint (2nd century B.C.) and Latin Vulgate (4th century A.D.) and many versions in the succeeding centuries. The memorial at Gilgal commemorated *what* happened, and the memorial in the River Jordan commemorated *where* it happened. Respect for God's Word necessitates that we accept as genuine the text that has come down to us.

In the past our nation's leaders have erected memorials to great men and women, and some memorials have commemorated events in our nation's history. For example, visitors to our nation's capital are shown the Lincoln Memorial, the Washington Monument, the Grave of the Unknown Soldier, and much more. These memorials serve as reminders of our heritage. And our calenders pinpoint other important events--Easter, Memorial Day, the Fourth of July, Reformation Sunday, Thanksgiving, Rosh Hashanah, Yom Kippur and Hanukkah, Christmas and New Year's Eve followed by New Year's Day--to name only a few. And to these events each of us adds the birthdays of those nearest and dearest to us, as well as our anniversary and the anniversaries of family members. All remind us of God's goodness.

Three Statements of Fact, 4:10-18. From these reminders of God's special intervention the biblical historian passes on to consider (1) Joshua's instructions to the priests (4:10-11, 15-18); (2) the faithfulness of the tribes of Reuben, Gad and Manasseh (4:12-13); and (3) the fulfillment of God's promise to Joshua (4:14).

During all the long day when the Israelites, young and old alike, crossed the Jordan, the priests had stood faithfully in the middle of the river bed. Joshua was mindful of their situation, and as soon as the last of the stones from the bank of the River Jordan had been placed on the river bed, he commanded them to come up onto the level plain facing Jericho. As soon as the soles of the priests' feet were safely on the west bank the Lord caused the waters to flow down as before. This indicates that the stopping of the river's flow was solely the result of divine power and not natural causes.

Earlier in the day 40,000 valiant men from the tribes of Reuben, Gad, and Manasseh had crossed the Jordan in the presence of their kinsmen. This was in accordance with the promise made to Moses months earlier. Others had remained in the areas allotted to them by Moses to guard the land, till the ground, and shepherd their flocks and herds.

Finally, in fulfillment of His promise (cf. 3:7), the Lord caused Joshua to stand high in the esteem of the people. After this they reverenced him in the same way they had reverenced Moses.

Two Reminders of God's Faithfulness, 4:19-24. It is interesting to note that the people of Israel had their anniversaries in much the same way we have ours. These special times included the fortieth anniversary of their Exodus from Egypt, and a visible reminder that would enable the people to teach their children this part of their history.

We read: "And the people came up out of the Jordan on the tenth day of the first month, and encamped in Gilgal, on the east border of Jericho. And those twelve stones, which they took out of the Jordan, Joshua set up in Gilgal. And he spoke to the children of Israel, saying, 'When your children shall ask their fathers in time to come, saying, "What mean these stones?" then you shall let your children know, saying, "Israel came over this Jordan on dry land. For Yahweh your God dried up the waters of the Jordan from before you, until you were passed over, as Yahweh your God did to the Red Sea, which he dried up from before us, until we were passed over; that all the peoples of the earth may know that the hand of Yahweh, is mighty; [and] that you may fear Yahweh your God forever." ' "

The date when the Israelites crossed the River Jordan was exactly forty years after the Exodus.[4] God had been faithful. This reminder of the past prepared the way for the

---

4. C. F. Keil and F. J. Delitzsch, "Joshua, Judges, Ruth," *Biblical Commentary on the Old Testament*, trans. J. Martin (Grand Rapids: Eerdmans, 1968), 51, state: "the crossing took place on the tenth day of the first month, that is to say, on the same day on which, forty years before, Israel had begun to prepare for going out of Egypt by setting apart the paschal lamb (Ex. xii.3)."

celebration of the Passover which we will read about in our next chapter. Though God had not punished the nation to excess for their sins (cf. Exodus 16:35; Numbers 14:33-34; 32:13), the unbelievers among them could not enter the Promised Land. They had lived and died in the desert. Now that their unbelief had been punished, the Lord moved to fulfill His promise to His people.

The second reminder of God's faithfulness took the form of an object lesson. The memorial that Joshua set up was designed to help parents instruct younger generations. In the future, when their children asked, "What do these stones mean?" parents would have the opportunity to recount to them the miraculous events of this important day. As Dr. George Bush has pointed out, "This would afford to parents an excellent opportunity to turn to account the inquisitiveness of their children, to make them early acquainted with the wonderful works of God, and to train them up in [reverence for Him]."[5]

All of this reminds us of the counsel Moses gave the Israelites before his death. He admonished parents to diligently teach their children, talking about the things of the Lord when they sat in their homes, walked along some path, and when they lay down or rose up (cf. Deuteronomy 6:6-7). Children are naturally inquisitive, and in this passage they are the ones who ask the question (4.21-24). The key to sound parenting is threefold: It is made up of *involvement, modeling, and instruction.* If our children have been reared in an atmosphere of respect, where they are encour-

---

5. Bush, *Joshua,* 52.

aged to voice their opinions, then their inquiring minds will lead them to ask questions; and each question will give us the opportunity to teach them truths they otherwise might not learn. Unfortunately we often look upon our children's questions as distractions from whatever we are doing, and so miss an opportunity to cultivate their God-given curiosity.

Further information about the parenting process is found in 4:23-24, and this highlights the importance of our instruction. All too often we look upon history as boring, for when we took history courses in school or college we were required to memorize endless dates and seemingly unrelated facts. Here, a father's teaching of his child was to be grounded in personal experience as well as a knowledge of the past (4:23); and what child will not sit with rapt attention as his father recounts in simple terms the trials faced by Odysseus as he tried repeatedly to get back to his beloved Penelope or the courage of the early pioneers as they opened up the western frontier.

Before we conclude our study of chapter 4, we should take note of the goal of our instruction. It involves the spread of the truth (4:24). Obviously this cannot take place overnight, but as our children grow toward adulthood, their winsome witness to the power and grace and lovingkindness of God should cause His name be "feared"[6] by all who hear of His mighty acts.

---

6. The "fear of the Lord" (i.e., living in *reverential awe* of God) involves two polar thoughts. The one is repulsion and the other is attraction. When Peter began to understand who the Lord Jesus is, he said, "Depart from me; for I am a sinful man, O Lord." Later on, when some of the disciples were leaving Christ, He asked the twelve, "Will you also go away." To this Peter answered, "Lord, to whom shall we go, for you have the words of eternal life" (cf. Luke 5:8; John 6:66-68). In these two statements we have the ideas of repulsion and attraction.

CHAPTER 5

PREPARING FOR CONQUEST

JOSHUA 5:1-15

Chapter 5 begins with, "Now it came about when all the kings of the Amorites who were beyond [i.e., the River] Jordan to the west, and all the kings of the Canaanites who were by the sea, heard how Yahweh had dried up the waters of the [River] Jordan before the sons of Israel until they had crossed, that their hearts melted, and there was no spirit in them any longer because of the sons of Israel."

As this verse is closely related to the events of chapter 4 (the crossing of the River Jordan), it would possibly have been better for it to conclude the crossing. Chapter and verse divisions in our Bibles, while of the utmost help, are not part of the original text and therefore are not inspired.

The inhabitants of Canaan were confident that the Jordan was a sufficient barrier to keep the Israelites at bay, at least for a time. Perhaps they were waiting to see if the Israelites would journey north or south and cross into Canaan at a more convenient place. But when the Lord dried up the waters and the Israelites began to cross, it was too late for them to form any alliances. They also remembered the events of the Red Sea and the destruction of Pharaoh's army, and deeming discretion to be the better part of valor, decided to stay inside their cities. Had they confronted the Israelites as they climbed up the bank of the River Jordan they might, humanly speaking, have repulsed them. God, however, saw to it that they were so filled with fear that none dared venture into open country.

The Circumcision of the People, 5:1-12

Among the treasured writings of Jonathan Edwards is his *Religious Affections* in which records his covenant to set Christ first in his life and to seek His glory above all else. It is no wonder that with such dedication to the Lord a spiritual awakening took place under his ministry, and many were brought to faith in Christ.

The Bible has a good deal to say about covenants. Sometimes it uses the word "vow" (cf. 1 Samuel 19-11; Psalms 22:25; 50:14, etc.). Both the Old and New Testaments refer to covenants between God and man, as well as between human beings (cf. Malachi 2:14). In the Old Testament the most common word for a covenant is *berit,* "to cut," and in the New Testament the term is *diatheke,* sometimes translated "testament" (cf. Hebrews 7:22; 9:15; 12:24).

In Joshua 5 we are reminded of the covenant of circumcision that God had instituted with Abraham centuries before the Israelites invaded Canaan (Genesis 17:9-14, noting esp. v.14). It involved the cutting off of the foreskin of the male genital organ, and in Hebrew/Jewish times this was done on the eighth day of a male child's life (cf. Leviticus 12:3; Luke 1:59; 2:21). The apostle Paul referred to this ancient practice as symbolic of the removal of the fleshly part of one's nature so that in Christ the believer may live his life to the glory of God (cf. Deuteronomy 10:16; 30:6; Romans 2:28-29).

To those of us who are Gentiles circumcision is looked upon as a medically advisable (but not essential) course of action, but among the Jews it is very significant. On the eighth day after a baby boy is born, he is circumcised and thereby becomes a member of the nation of Israel and inherits all the blessings of the Abrahamic covenant (Romans 3:1-2).

With the Israelites having successfully invaded the land of Canaan, we would have expected Joshua to launch an attack on Jericho without delay. Instead of attacking the city, he gave instructions for all uncircumcised males to be circumcised. This command came from the Lord. We read:

"At that time Yahweh said to Joshua, 'Make for yourself flint knives and circumcise again the sons of Israel the second time.'[1] So Joshua made himself flint knives and circumcised the sons of Israel at Gibeath-haaraloth. This is the reason why circumcision was necessary: all the males who came out of Egypt who were men of war, died in the wilderness along the way after they came out of Egypt. For all the people who came out were circumcised, but all the people who were born in the wilderness along the way as they came out of Egypt had not been circumcised. For the

---

1. Circumcision was also practiced by other Near Eastern races, see J. M. Sasson, *Journal of Biblical Literature* 85 (1966), 473-76, and *Ancient Near Eastern Texts Relating to the Old Testament*, ed. J. B. Pritchard, 2d ed., (Princeton: Princeton U. P., 1955), 326.

sons of Israel walked forty years in the wilderness, until all the nation, that is, the men of war who came out of Egypt, perished because they did not listen to the voice of Yahweh, to whom Yahweh had sworn that He would not let them see the land which Yahweh had sworn to their fathers to give us, a land flowing with milk and honey. Their children whom He raised up in their place, Joshua circumcised; for they were uncircumcised, because they had not circumcised them along the way. Now when they had finished circumcising all the nation, they remained in their places in the camp until they were healed. Then Yahweh said to Joshua, 'Today I have rolled away the reproach of Egypt from you.' So the name of that place is called Gilgal to this day."

From a practical point of view we might ask, "If circumcision was so important, why didn't Joshua have the men undergo this rite during the period of relative inactivity while they were camping on the other side of the River Jordan, and the Jordan offered them some protection?" The answer has been supplied by the great Scottish Bible teacher, Dr. William G. Blaikie. He reminds us that at Kadesh-Barnea, when the Israelites believed the report of the ten spies and doubted God's ability to give them the land (Numbers 13-14, noting in particular 14:1-4), the adult generation that had come out of Egypt was excluded from Canaan and in the thirty-eight years that followed they perished in the wilderness. Their disbelief in God's faithfulness also resulted in the suspension of circumcision which involved belief in the covenant.[2]

---

2. Blaikie, *Joshua*, 118-19.

For the taking of Canaan to be successful the people under Joshua must be in a right relationship with God, and so all those who had not previously been circumcised now submitted to this rite.

Dr. Blaikie remarks, "We may well think of it (i.e., circumcision) as an occasion of great rejoicing. The visible token of being one of God's children was now borne by every man and boy in the camp. In a sense they now regarded themselves as heirs of the covenant made with their fathers."[3]

But what are we to understand by God's statement that the "reproach" of Egypt had been removed? In Egypt the Israelites had been a nation of slaves. Now they were heirs to the promises God had made with their fathers (cf. Genesis 17:1-14), and had begun to take possession of the land. This served as a sufficient rebuke to those Egyptians who, during Israel's wandering in the desert, had told them that their God was incapable of bringing them into the land.

---

3. Ibid, 119. Bush (*Joshua,* 58-59) offers a slightly different interpretation: "Their bondage in Egypt was, in a sense, a reproach and a disgrace to them; it would be so accounted by other nations, while it continued, and they would be disparaged by reason of it. It is probable also that the Egyptians themselves, seeing them wander so long in the wilderness, reproached and taunted them, as if brought there to be destroyed; but now, having entered Canaan in triumph, and being put in possession of the covenanted blessing promised to the seed of Abraham, of which circumcision was the seal, this reproach was henceforth done away."

The second rite observed by the Israelites was the Passover. "While the sons of Israel camped at Gilgal they observed the Passover on the evening of the fourteenth day of the month on the desert plains of Jericho. On the day after the Passover, on that very day, they ate some of the produce of the land, unleavened cakes and parched grain. The manna ceased on the day after they had eaten some of the produce of the land, so that the sons of Israel no longer had manna, but they ate some of the yield of the land of Canaan during that year."

The celebration of the first Passover in Egypt was in anticipation of their emancipation. Now, as the Israelites observed the Passover in Canaan, they looked back to God's great interposition on their behalf and drew fresh hope for the future. In a similar way our observance of the Lord's Table causes us to look back in faith to Christ's death on the cross for our redemption and forward in hope to the time of His glorious return (Colossians 3:4).

We are also told that at this time the Israelites ate the "old corn" of the land. After the Passover the Israelites ate unleavened cakes and parched corn. Then the manna[4] ceased. The miracle of God's providential supply was discontinued when it was no longer necessary. The manna had been given them in the desert where a sufficient quantity of food could not be found. But now that they were in their

---

4. For a discussion of the nature and appearance of the manna, see Robinson, *Biblical Researches*, I:470, 550; Tristham, *Natural History of the Bible*, 362; and Kitto, *Daily Bible Illustrations*, I:480-81.

own land with fields and orchards and vineyards, the manna was withdrawn.

This illustrates for us an important principle in God's economy. He has promised to supply our needs (Philippians 4:19), but this does not exclude personal effort. If we have the ability to earn enough money to buy food then we should not expect that it be supplied in supernatural ways. In other words, we cannot look for God's blessing without diligent use of His appointed means.

The Commander of the Lord's Army, 5:13-15

A great deal had happened in the two weeks since the crossing of the River Jordan. Joshua now anticipated the attack on Jericho, and went out to gain some firsthand knowledge of the strength of the city. So far no divine communication had come to him, and so he looked intently at Jericho wondering what strategy he should use. The Lord erased his concerns, for we read: "Now it came about when Joshua was by Jericho that he lifted up his eyes and looked, and behold, a man was standing opposite him with his sword drawn in his hand, and Joshua went to him and said to him, 'Are you for us or for our adversaries?' He said, 'No; rather I indeed come now as captain of Yahweh's host.' And Joshua fell on his face to the earth, and bowed down, and asked, 'What has my lord to say to his servant?' The captain of Yahweh's host said to Joshua, 'Remove your sandals from your feet, for the place where you are standing is holy.' And Joshua did so."

This "man" is expressly referred to as Yahweh in 6:2. His appearance was an "anthropomorphism"--the manifestation of the Lord Jesus in human form. We may be confident of this by what follows. He refers to Himself as the "Captain of the Host of the Lord," implying that He is the ruler of the armies of heaven. He also accepted Joshua's worship. Were He a created being He would not have permitted such veneration. And instead of reproving Joshua, He commanded him to remove his sandals thus insisting upon the highest human acknowledgment.[5]

It is important for us to notice that the Lord Jesus had a drawn sword in His hand. This indicates the character He now assumed (cf. the reference to Him as a "man of war" in Exodus 15:3). His people were to embark on a mission that would involve the capture of the entire land, and if He was for them, who could be against them?

The Lord Jesus had appeared in different forms at different times. He had appeared as Yahweh to Moses in the burning bush (Exodus 3), as the Angel of the Lord during Israel's wanderings (Exodus 23:23), and now He appeared as the Leader of God's armies and Defender of God's covenant people. His character is reflected in the different names given Him, and here He comes as the Lord of the heavenly and earthly armies.

Joshua's response is most fitting: "What does my Lord have to say to His servant?" In Joshua's prostrate form and words of profound reverence we see his complete submis-

---

5. Bush, *Joshua*, 61.

sion to the Lord as the Leader of the campaign which is about to begin. And with that the Lord gives him the instructions that are contained in our next chapter.

As we review what we have covered in this chapter it is appropriate for us to consider any abiding lessons that are inherent in the text. Of the many, we will consider only four: The Need for Obedience, The Importance if Priorities, The Place of Remembrance, and The Presence of the Lord.

The Need for Obedience. A wise Christian once remarked "Every great person has first learned how to obey, whom to obey, and when to obey." This was true of Joshua. His many years of leadership under Moses had taught him many things. Now, however, Canaan lay before God's people, but the Jordan River rolled between. Joshua had inspired the people's trust and so when he commanded them to come down to Jordan's bank, they did so. They believed that God, in some special way, would make a way for them through the river. And He did. Though God may not always cause our obstacles to disappear, He is still sovereign and we can trust Him to do whatever is necessary for us so that we may do His will.

The Importance of Priorities. Once within the borders of the Promised Land we would have expected the people to proceed immediately to attack, namely the conquest of Jericho. Instead the male Hebrews who had not previously been circumcised submitted to this rite. They needed to be in a covenant relationship with the Lord. Scripture does not say that after keeping God's commandments there is great reward, but in keeping them there is great reward. Obedience to God's revealed will precedes the receiving of His blessing.

The Place of Remembrance. Some churches are ritualistic. It seems as if they continually live in the past. There is a place for remembrance and these occasions are clearly spelled out in Scripture. Israel had its feast days, and the Church today has its celebration of the Lord's Table. These events should not be celebrated so frequently that they lose their meaning. But when they do occur we should make the most of them. Israel in Canaan celebrated the Passover, and it was a time of thankfulness to the Lord who had redeemed them from those who persecuted them. Finally, there is the reminder of ...

The Presence of the Lord. As the Israelites faced the challenge of taking possession of the Promised Land, the Lord Jesus appeared to Joshua and assured him of His presence. And He is with us, too, for He said, "Lo, I am with you always even to the end of the age" (Matthew 28:20). What glorious assurance! Every moment of every day He is with us, and so we should never be afraid to speak to Him in prayer or call upon Him for help (Hebrews 13:6).

CHAPTER 6

THE CAPTURE OF JERICHO

JOSHUA 6:1-27

The time for the conquest of Canaan had finally arrived. What strategy would Joshua use? Jericho was well fortified. It had double walls protecting its inhabitants. How could the Israelites gain access into the city?

Some years ago a spiritual became very popular with young children at summer camps and during Vacation Bible School. It was *Joshua Fit*[1] *de Battle of Jericho*. The song went like this:

> Joshua fit de battle of Jericho, Jericho, Jericho,
> Joshua fit de battle of Jericho
> and de walls came tumbling down....
>
> Up to de walls of Jericho
> He marched with spear in hand,
> Go blow dem ram-horns," Joshua cried,
> "Cause de battle is in my hand."
>
> Then de lamp-ram sheep-horn begin to blow,

---

1. I.e., Fought.

Trumpets begin to sound,
Joshua commanded de children to shout
and de walls came tumbling down....
Anonymous.

The story of the victory God gave the Israelites over the people of Jericho is not only pertinent to young children, its lessons of *faith and obedience* are for all ages.

OUTLINE

In chapters 1–5 we focused our attention on the entrance of the Israelites into the Promised Land. Now, beginning with chapter 6, we will consider how the land was conquered. Chapters 6–12 may be divided as follows:

The Conquest of Central Canaan, 6:1–8:35
The Conquest of Southern Canaan, 9:1–10:43
The Conquest of Northern Canaan, 11:1-15
A Summary of the Conquest, 11:16–12:24.

THE CONQUEST OF CENTRAL CANAAN, 6:1–8:35

The Victory Is the Lord's, 6:1-27

In early times battering rams were used to break down gates leading into a city; and, simultaneously mounds were erected against city walls so that soldiers could easily surmount them and gain access into a stronghold. Would Joshua give the order for them to begin building these time-tested ways so that they could penetrate this strongly fortified city?[2]

From what we read in chapter 6 the Lord had other ideas. "Yahweh said to Joshua, 'See, *I have given*[3] Jericho into your hand, with its king and the valiant warriors. You shall march around the city, all the men of war circling the city once. You shall do so for six days. Also, seven priests shall carry seven trumpets of rams' horns before the ark; then on the seventh day you shall march around the city seven times,[4] and the priests shall blow the trumpets. It shall be that when they make a long blast with the ram's horn, and when you hear the sound of the trumpet, all the people shall shout with a great shout; and the wall of the city will fall down flat, and the people will go up every man straight ahead.'"

"So Joshua the son of Nun called the priests and said to them, 'Take up the Ark of the Covenant, and let seven priests carry seven trumpets of rams' horns before the Ark of Yahweh.' Then he said to the people, 'Go forward, and march around the city, and let the armed men go on before the Ark of Yahweh.'"

---

2. J. J. Niehaus, *Journal of the Evangelical Theological Society* 31 (1988), 37-50.
3. A prophetic perfect tense. Victory was assured.
4. Archaeologists have estimated that Jericho covered an area of approximately 8.5 acres. It could easily be circled seven times on the seventh day. See M. Avi-Yonah, ed., *Encyclopedia of Archaeological Excavations in the Holy Land* (Englewood Cliffs, NJ: Prentice-Hall, 1976), II:550-75.

"And it was so, that when Joshua had spoken to the people, the seven priests carrying the seven trumpets of rams' horns before Yahweh went forward and blew the trumpets; and the Ark of the Covenant of the Lord followed them. The armed men went before the priests who blew the trumpets, and the rear guard came after the Ark, while they continued to blow the trumpets."

We may well ask, What kind of strategy was this? What was to prevent the men of Jericho from charging out of each of Jericho's gates to attack the line of Israelites, thus separating one group from another, and inflicting heavy casualties on each? Then, if the fighting became too much for them they could withdraw toward the city and the archers on the wall could further decimate Israel's fighting men.

True faith trusts God implicitly. The Lord did not say "I shall give Jericho into your hand," but "I have given it into your hand." He not only will do it, but as far as He is concerned it is as good as done. The outcome is sure. Our obedience is all that is required to make this promise a reality.

From a human point of view, walking around the city seemed to be the height of insanity. And whoever heard of the thick walls of a city falling down just because people shouted?[5] In my youth I was taught that if Christians would surround their problems with prayer the difficulties they faced would "fall down flat"in the same way the walls of the city of Jericho had collapsed before the Israelites. This teaching was applied specifically to missions with the expectation that the "walls" of heathenism would crumble before the prayers of God's people. Unfortunately the proponents of this teaching did not go back to the text of Scripture to verify that this is what the passage taught. Joshua had said to the people, "You shall not shout nor let your voice be heard nor let a word proceed out of your mouth, until the day I tell you, 'Shout!' Then you shall shout!"

Happily for us there are verses in the New Testament that do encourage us to pray for ourselves as well as for others, but to use the conquest of Jericho as an example of successful prayer is to stretch the teaching of this passage. What is remarkable is the combination of faith and obedience on the part of the priests and the people (cf. Hebrews 11:30). And faith in the overriding providence of God gave the Israelites confidence that the soldiers in Jericho would not sally forth and engage them in battle while they were marching around the city.

For six days the Israelites marched around Jericho in silence. Perhaps the only sounds came from those lining the walls of Jericho. After their initial shock the first day they probably gained courage and as each successive day witnessed the same routine, they may have begun jeering at

---

5. The wall was approximately thirty feet high. The part of the wall on which Rahab's house had been built did not collapse. Most writers believe that the walls fell down because of an earthquake. If so, then the quake occurred at precisely the time the men uttered their war cry (which would be a remarkable miracle of timing). The Israelite encampment approximately 1.5 miles away was unaffected, and the sheep and cattle did not panic or stampede.

their opponents (as was the custom in those days when armies faced each other prior to a battle).

On the seventh day God's people marched around the city seven times. Then Joshua gave the order: "Shout! For Yahweh has given you the city. The city shall be under the ban, it and all that is in it belongs to Yahweh;[6] only Rahab the harlot and all who are with her in the house shall live, because she hid the messengers whom we sent. But as for you, only keep yourselves from the things under the ban, so that you do not covet them and take some of the things under the ban, and make the camp of Israel accursed and bring trouble on it. But all the silver and gold and articles of bronze and iron are holy to Yahweh; they shall go into the treasury of Yahweh"[7] (6:16-19).

We can imagine the consternation of the people inside Jericho. The regular routine of a single march around their

---

6. Scholars have doubted and debated the destruction of Jericho for decades. Most do not believe it happened the way the Bible describes. In spite of arguments to the contrary there is archaeological evidence that the outer wall fell down the slope of the hill on which Jericho had been built. The inner wall fell into the gap between the walls. For a summary of the evidence, see L. J. Wood, *A Survey of Israel's History* (Grand Rapids: Zondervan, 1970), 173-75.
7. How did those on the other side of Jericho, who could not see Joshua, hear what he said? It is probable that the fighting men moved out in accordance with the positions of their tribes when they began their march through the desert. If so, then their leaders could easily have relayed Joshua's command to the men under their command.

city had been changed. With each additional circuit their apprehension must have grown. Each one knew that this was the day they would have to face the Israelites in hand-to-hand combat.

When the people heard Joshua's command to shout, they "shouted, and priests blew the trumpets ... and the wall fell down flat, so that the people went up into the city, every man straight ahead, and they took the city. They utterly destroyed everything in the city, both man and woman, young and old, and ox and sheep and donkey, with the edge of the sword" (6:19-20). The Lord had given them the city (cf. 2 Chronicles 14:11), and in accordance with the command of the Lord, Joshua and the men of Israel burned the city.

But why did God command the annihilation of the people?[8] There are two major answers given this question. The first of which is both religious and social. A little more than four centuries earlier God had told Abraham that after the captivity of His people in Egypt He would bring them out and use them to judge the Amorites and Canaanites for their sins (Genesis 15:16). But what were the sins of these races? Infant sacrifices to their gods, and sexual immorality of every kind were their most prominent offenses. To prevent social diseases from spreading to His people, and to minimize the temptation of Israelites worshiping the depraved

---

8. D. M. Howard, Jr., *Joshua*, New American Commentary (Nashville: Broadman & Holman, 1998), 180-87. See also M. F.. Unger, *Archaeology and the Old Testament* (Grand Rapids: Zondervan, 1966), 169-77.

gods of Canaan, the Lord ordered the extermination of the people. The second reason was to prevent a future fortress from being built on that mound that would prevent the Israelites from having direct access to the interior of Canaan (see 6:26).

Only Rahab and her family were spared (6:17, 22-25). Joshua gave specific instructions for the promise made to her by the spies to be carried out. "The city shall be under the ban, it and all that is in it belongs to Yahweh; only Rahab the harlot and all who are with her in the house shall live, because she hid the messengers whom we sent.... [Then] Joshua said to the two men who had spied out the land, 'Go into the harlot's house and bring the woman and all she has out of there, as you have sworn to her.'[9] So the young men who were spies went in and brought out Rahab and her father and her mother and her brothers and all she had; they also brought out all her relatives and *placed them outside the camp of Israel*.... Rahab the harlot and her father's household and all she had, Joshua spared; and she has lived *in the midst of Israel* to this day, for she hid the messengers whom Joshua sent to spy out Jericho" (emphasis added).

Only Rahab exhibited a spirit of contrition.[10] No one else in Jericho turned in faith to Israel's God. How remarkable was her faith? In the "golden roll" of Hebrews 11 she

---

9. Free, *Archaeology and Bible History*, 130-32.
10. If we may borrow a thought from 1 Corinthians 7:14, Rahab's family was placed in a position of blessing because of her.

is the only woman to share with Sarah the honor of being placed among the heroes of faith. Her identification with God's people changed her life. Without a doubt she underwent some ritual by which she was included within the people of Israel, and in time she married Salmon who was from the tribe of Judah (Matthew 1:5).

Dr. William Blaikie summed up the story in this way: "When the enemy ensnares a woman, wiles her into the filthiest chambers of sin, and so enchains her there that she cannot escape, but must sink deeper and deeper into the mire, the case is truly hopeless. More rapidly and more thoroughly than in the case of man, the 'leprosy' (of her immoral lifestyle) spreads till every virtuous principle is rooted out, and every womanly feeling is displaced .... Is there any art to breathe the breath of purity and pure love into that defiled soul?... By the grace of God the sinner can be restored. The Lord Jesus can restore the one who turns from her sins. To such He says, 'You are washed, you are sanctified, you are justified by the Spirit of God.'"[11]

In the conquest of Jericho we see God's justice in punishing sin as well as His mercy in sparing Rahab and her family. We also note in a very practical way the vital connection between trust (i.e., faith) and obedience. There is a beautiful hymn that amplifies this point. It was written by John H. Sammis (1846-1919).

---

11. Blaikie, *Joshua*, 153-63.

When we walk with the Lord in the light of His Word,
what a glory He sheds on our way!
While we do His good will He abides with us still,
and with all who will trust and obey.
Not a shadow can rise, not a cloud in the skies,
but His smile quickly drives it away;
Not a doubt nor a fear, not a sigh nor a tear,
can abide while we trust and obey.
Not a burden we bear, not a sorrow we share,
but our toil He doth richly repay;
Not a grief not a loss, not a frown nor a cross,
but is blest if we trust and obey.
But we never can prove the delights of His love
until all on the altar we lay,
For the favor He shows and the joy He bestows
are for them who will trust and obey.
Then in fellowship sweet we will sit at His feet,
or we'll walk by His side in the way;
What He says we will do, where He sends we will go–
Never fear, only trust and obey.

The account of the salvation of Rahab and her family is a remarkable story of God's grace!

CHAPTER 7

RESTORING GOD'S FAVOR

JOSHUA 7:1-26

Some years ago my wife and sons and I vacationed at Wisconsin Dells. One sunny day we took a motor launch up the river. As we rounded a rocky knoll, we saw that one of the other motorboats had become stuck in a submerged mud bank. The pilot of the stranded vessel had taken a corner too sharply, and the prow had become firmly fixed in the mud. The pilot was greatly embarrassed and, as we found out later, he had already radioed for another launch to come and take his passengers on their tour.

After completing our excursion we headed down river where we again passed the stranded launch. There we saw that another boat had attached a cable to the stricken vessel, and with engines at full throttle, was trying to free the grounded craft from the bank.

The tendency to cut corners–ethical, spiritual, material and social–is widespread. When this happens the progress we are making toward a specific goal or objective may come to a sudden halt. Difficulties arise from an unexpected source, and try as we might, we cannot overcome the obstacles that bar our way.

In the Bible we have an account of such an occurrence. Joshua 7:1 begins with an ominous *"But ...."* The importance attached to this incident is evident from the amount of space devoted to it, and the truths we can learn from this story can be applied to a variety of circumstances.

As we look back, we remind ourselves that in chapter 6 the Lord gave His people a great victory. The people of Jericho were resoundingly defeated. Now, in chapter 7, we read of their ignominious defeat before those living in the small town of Ai.[1] Why did God's people fail?

DEFEAT AT AI

God's Anger Aroused, 7:1

For the answer to Israel's failure we need to take a careful look at the biblical text. "But the sons of Israel acted unfaithfully in regard to the things under the ban, for Achan, the son of Carmi, the son of Zabdi, the son of Zerah, from the tribe of Judah, took some of the things under the ban, therefore the anger of Yahweh burned against the sons of Israel."

The spoil from Jericho was to be dedicated to the Lord as the firstfruits of Israel's conquest of the land.[2] Joshua

---

1. There is considerable debate over the identification of Ai and Bethel. The identification of Ai as et-Tell cannot be maintained, for the site was uninhabited between 2200 and 1200 B.C. See *Encyclopedia of Archaeological Excavations in the Holy Land* (1975), I:36-52.

had specifically warned the Israelites not to take anything that was under the ban (i.e., consecrated to the Lord) when he gave the army their orders. As God's theocratic leader[3] his instructions were to be obeyed. They were also clear: "But as for you, only keep yourselves from the things under the ban, so that you do not covet them and take some of the things under the ban, and make the camp of Israel accursed and bring trouble on it. But all the silver and gold and articles of bronze and iron are holy to Yahweh; they shall go into Yahweh's treasury" (6:18-19).

That night, however, when the other Israelites were celebrating the victory around their camp fires, Achan (the subject of our story) had crept stealthily back to the smoldering ruins of Jericho. There he located the spot where he had hidden some silver and gold and a beautiful cloak made in land of Shinar (i.e., Babylon). Then, with heart pounding, he had returned to his tent where he dug a hole in the ground and hid his loot.[4]

---

2. Howard, *Joshua,* 180-87, has an excellent excursus on *herem* and the need for consecration.
3. "Theocracy" comes from two Greek words, *Theos,* "God," and *kratein,* "to rule," and looks at those people specifically set apart by God who speak and act on His behalf.
4. Achan's family must have been aware of what he did, and thus became his accomplices (cf. Deuteronomy 24:16).

Israel's Attack on Ai, 7:2-5

"Now Joshua sent men from Jericho to Ai, which is near Beth-aven, east of Bethel[5], and said to them, 'Go up and spy out the land.' So the men went up and spied out Ai[6]. They returned to Joshua and said to him, 'Do not let all the people go up; only about two or three thousand men need go up to Ai; do not make all the people toil up there, for they are few.' So about three thousand men from the people went up there, but they fled from the men of Ai. The men of Ai struck down about thirty-six of them, and pursued them from the gate as far as Shebarim and struck them down on the descent, so the hearts of the people melted and became as water."

There are several specifics that we need to note as we consider what Joshua and the spies did. First, Joshua did not ask counsel from the Lord. He presumed that the Lord was with him, but the "Captain of the Host of the Lord" was apparently not around to give Joshua any specific instructions. Second, the men sent to reconnoiter Ai were self-reliant. They looked solely at the size of the city and concluded that, when compared to Jericho, this city would not give

---

5. The identification of Bethel is also the subject of debate. D. Livingstone in the *Palestine Exploration Quarterly* (1994), 154-59, believes biblical Bethel is el-Bireh, but his research has been rejected by B. K. Waltke, *Westminster Theological Quarterly* 52 (1990), 193. See also *Encyclopedia of Archaeological Excavations in the Holy Land,* I:190-93.
6. About 15 miles from Jericho and strategically located in the central hill country.

them any trouble. In their opinion it did not warrant the efforts of all Israel's fighting force.

The mistake made by the spies is one that has been repeated over and over again. In our churches we conclude that the people should not be burdened with all the work, but that it should be left to a few, or to the pastor (for, after all, he's paid to do the work). And then we're surprised when the work of the church begins to falter. Acts 6:4 makes it clear that a pastor's responsibility is to devote himself to prayer and the ministry of the Word! Other work is to be done by the members of the church.

In Israel's case the sin of disobedience had caused the Lord to withdraw His presence, and the men sent to attack Ai met with a resounding defeat. We are told that the men of Ai chased them from the gate of the city (where the Israelites may have been trying to light a fire to burn it down) all the way to *hash-shebarim*, "the breaches"--possibly a declivity in the hill leading down to the valley and safety. Not all the Israelites could enter this narrow defile at once and so thirty-six of their number were killed while trying to escape.

As word of the defeat spread through the camp at Gilgal the people became filled with fear. They knew that as soon as the Canaanites became aware of what had happened they would gain confidence, join forces, and wage a stern war against Israel. (Cf. what David's enemies said at a later time, Psalm 71:11).

Joshua's Astonished Response, 7:6-9

The effect of the defeat on Joshua was overwhelming. "Then Joshua tore his clothes and fell to the earth on his face before the Ark of Yahweh until the evening, both he and the elders of Israel; and they put dust on their heads. Joshua said, 'Alas, O Yahweh God, why did You ever bring this people over the Jordan, only to deliver us into the hand of the Amorites, to destroy us?[7] If only we had been willing to dwell beyond the Jordan! O Lord, what can I say since Israel has turned their back before their enemies? For the Canaanites and all the inhabitants of the land will hear of it, and they will surround us and cut off our name from the earth. And what will You do for Your great name?'"

To rend one's clothes and throw dust onto one's head was a sign of intense grief and anguish. In the case of Joshua and the elders of Israel they also indicate their humility and despair.

Joshua's prayer revealed his true humanity. He grieved the loss of thirty-six men, and he was bewildered by Israel's defeat. Hadn't God promised him victory over his enemies? Why then had Israel been foiled in their plans to take Ai? Did the fault lie with him--in a sin of either omission or

---

7. Joshua and the elders of Israel were filled with fear. Fear attributes to a person, place or thing two attributes that properly belong to God: almightiness (the power to take away our autonomy) and impendency (the power to do us harm). The only real antidote to fear is to place ourselves unreservedly in God's sovereign care.

commission? The debacle at Ai had made Israel's position precarious, for the other inhabitants of Canaan would learn of Ai's success, surround God's people, and wipe them off the face of the earth. Then what would become of God's promises?

Joshua remained before the Lord until evening.

God's Stern Explanation, 7:10-12a

"So Yahweh said to Joshua, 'Rise up! Why is it that you have fallen on your face? *Israel has sinned*, and they have also transgressed My covenant which I commanded them. And they have even taken some of the things under the ban and have both stolen and deceived. Moreover, they have also put them among their own things. Therefore the sons of Israel cannot stand before their enemies; they turn their backs before their enemies, for they have become accursed" (emphasis added).

Possibly at 3:00 P.M., the time of the evening sacrifice, God broke the cycle of Joshua's despair. His words were stern: "Get up! Why have you fallen on your face? Israel has sinned ...."[8] So that was the reason. But would God withdraw His blessings from all the people because of the sin of one individual? Yes. We, being Occidentals, are inclined to think in terms of individual responsibility, and ignore the corporate entity; but God's people, having an Oriental frame of mind, were accustomed to thinking in

---

8. Cf. H. W. Robinson's *Corporate Personality in Ancient Israel*, revised ed. (Philadelphia: Fortress, 1980), 64pp.

terms of the community. What one person did affected them all. That is why God said, "Israel has sinned."

We, however, cannot shrug off the teaching of this passage by offering as our excuse, "But we're Gentiles." When the apostle Paul wrote the believers in Rome he stated that "no man lives for himself, and no man dies for himself" (Romans 14:7). We are bound together in the "bundle of life." Absolute independence and isolation are impossible. A son's conduct reflects on his parents. A father's actions involve his family. A daughter's behavior mirrors her parents. A mother's standards are reproduced in the home. And unconfessed sin in the church causes a blunting of the church's vision and a lessening of the impact of its ministry. In the case of Achan, his sin rendered the whole nation powerless.

God's Ultimatum, 7:12b

God's ultimatum was clear: "I will not be with you anymore unless you destroy the things under the ban from your midst." Israel had, by their iniquity, placed themselves outside the realm of the covenant and the protection it afforded, and unless this matter was rectified God's blessing would not be restored.

We do well to ponder this situation so that we may better understand how God views sin in our lives.

God's Gracious Directive, 7:13-15

God's command to Joshua left no room for misunderstanding. "Rise up! Consecrate the people and say, 'Consecrate yourselves for tomorrow, for thus Yahweh, the God of Israel, has said, "There are things under the ban in your midst, O Israel. You cannot stand before your enemies until you have removed the things under the ban from your midst." In the morning then you shall come near by your tribes, and it shall be that the tribe which Yahweh takes by lot[9] shall come near by families, and the family which Yahweh takes shall come near by households, and the household which Yahweh takes shall come near man by man. It shall be that the one who is taken with the things under the ban shall be burned with fire, he and all that belongs to him, because he has transgressed the covenant of Yahweh, and because he has committed a disgraceful thing in Israel.'"

The situation was serious. Each person was to prepare himself for examination by a holy and all-knowing Judge. The consecration called for involved the washing of each person's clothes as well as his/her body. And such an external rite possibly also induced many to examine their own hearts and pray in much the same way as the psalmist, when he said:

---

9. The "casting of lots" was an ancient method of determining God's will (cf. 7:14). See especially Proverbs 16:33. See also 1 Samuel 10:20-21; 14:41-42; Acts 1:24, 26.

"Search me, O God, and know my heart;
Try me and know my anxious thoughts;
And see if there be any hurtful way in me,
And lead me in the everlasting way"
(Psalm 139:23-24).

Of course, Achan may have excused his early actions in taking things under the ban by reasoning within himself, "What harm will it do? I'm really doing this for my wife and family. And after all, we've been poor long enough. There are others in my tribe who are no older than I am, and their wives and children enjoy all of the things my loved ones are denied. Now is my opportunity to improve our situation" But who can tabulate the misery of those thirty-six homes bereaved of a husband and father? Who can calculate the unhappiness and loneliness of those so recently made widows and orphans? How could Achan remedy the situation of a boy growing to manhood without the leadership of a father, or of a young bride being deprived of the security and affection of her husband, or of a mother facing old age without the comfort of a son?

Achan possibly did little more than toss about that night. A feeling of discomfort, partly caused by fear and partly the result of guilt, probably kept him from enjoying a night of real rest. Feelings of uneasiness, however, were not sufficiently strong to motivate him to make his way through the darkness to Joshua's tent and confess what he had done. Had he done so, mercy might have been extended to him. Instead he tried in vain to find comfort amid the rugs that formed the bed he and his family lay on.

Joshua's Prompt Response, 7:16-18

The next morning dawned much the same as other mornings, only now Achan's misgivings could not be dismissed. He had no appetite to eat anything even though his stomach was empty and growled its discomfort. His mouth was dry. All he could do was wait for the summons to assemble before the Tent of the Lord with other members of his tribe.

We read that Joshua "arose early in the morning and brought Israel near by tribes, and the tribe of Judah was taken. (Achan may have felt like running away, but his legs seemed to be made of lead and would not move.) Next Joshua brought the tribe of Judah near, and he took the family of the Zerahites. (By now Achan's palms were probably sweaty and his face was pale). Joshua brought the family of the Zerahites near man by man, and Zabdi was taken. (The noose was beginning to tighten, and Achan felt his heart pounding loudly in his chest). Joshua brought Zabdi's household near man by man; and Achan, son of Carmi, son of Zabdi, son of Zerah, from the tribe of Judah, was taken."

On wobbly legs Achan stumbled forward, hoping that the earth would open up and swallow him as it did Dathan and Abiram (Numbers 16:28-32). The stares of his fellow Israelites were devoid of pity. Then, before he knew how he got there, he was standing before Joshua.

Achan's Sin Exposed and Punished, 7:19-25

Joshua spoke kindly to Achan. "My son, I implore you, give glory to Yahweh, the God of Israel, and give praise to Him; and tell me now what you have done. Do not hide it from me." (Only Joshua knew what Achan had done. Others may have thought him guilty of some act of idolatry, or some unhallowed sensuality like that which had occurred at Baal-peor [Numbers 25:1-9; Deuteronomy 4:3]). So Joshua appealed to Achan to confess his sin.

Achan answered Joshua and said, "Truly, I have sinned against Yahweh, the God of Israel, and this is what I did: When *I saw* among the spoil a beautiful mantle from Shinar and two hundred shekels of silver and a bar of gold fifty shekels in weight, then *I coveted* them and [*I*] *took* them; and behold, they are concealed in the earth inside my tent with the silver underneath it" (emphasis added).

The apostle John told us that temptation comes to us in three ways, through "the lust of the flesh (what I want to do), the lust of the eyes (what I want to have), and the pride of life (what I want to be)" (1 John 2:16). Achan saw some of the spoils of war and took them, even though he knew that they belonged to the Lord.

"So Joshua sent messengers, and they ran to the tent; and behold, it was concealed in his tent with the silver underneath it. They took them from inside the tent and brought them to Joshua and to all the sons of Israel, and they poured them out before Yahweh."

Achan's confession, though not made until it was extorted, told the whole story. Pale and trembling, he made no attempt to cover up his sin. Scripture warns us that our sins will find us out (cf. Numbers 32:23; see also Ecclesiastes 12:14; Amos 9:3), and this truth is illustrated in a dramatic way in what happened to Achan. "Then Joshua and all Israel with him, took Achan the son of Zerah, the silver, the mantle, the bar of gold, his sons, his daughters, his oxen, his donkeys, his sheep, his tent and all that belonged to him; and they brought them up to the valley of Achor. Joshua said, 'Why have you troubled us? Yahweh will trouble you this day.' And all Israel stoned them with stones; and they burned *them* with fire after they had stoned them with stones" (emphasis added).

Did Achan's family share his fate? They had been in the tent with him when he buried what he had retrieved from the ruins of Jericho.

There are many who try to drive a wedge between the "God of the Old Testament" and the "God of the New Testament." They claim that the "God of the Old Testament" is harsh, despotic, and devoid of the grace and compassion we encounter in the New Testament. And, of course, they point to incidents like the supposed killing of Achan's children to "prove" their point.

The Bible's critics, however, become the victims of their own malice. Joshua was a godly man. He had been the close confidant of Moses for forty years. He spent time each day meditating on God's Word. He knew the teaching of Deuteronomy 24:16 that children were not to be punished for the sins of their parents.

The Jewish rabbis who gave us the Talmud explained Joshua 7:25 to mean that all Israel stoned Achan, and then burned his dead body with the things that he had stolen. Achan's sons and daughters were taken to the place of execution as witnesses.[10]

God's Anger Assuaged, 7:26

With sin having been decisively dealt with, "they raised over Achan a great heap of stones that stands to this day, and Yahweh turned from the fierceness of His anger. Therefore the name of that place has been called the valley of Achor (i.e., "Trouble") to this day."

Some writers believe that the location of Achor was a small ravine at the end of a valley. If this is so, then the story ends on a note of poetic justice, for the Israelites killed by the men of Ai had perished in a similar gully after being routed by the enemy.

This story is more than an account of human tragedy, for there are some timeless truths to be derived from this chapter. James informs us that we cut corners–ethical, spiritual, personal–when we are carried away and enticed by our own lust; and that when lust has been conceived in our hearts it gives birth to sin; and sin when it is finished, brings forth death (James 1:14-15).

---

10. *The Talmud*, Sanhedrin, 44a.

CHAPTER 8

THE CAPTURE OF AI

JOSHUA 8:1-35

When we think of Frank Sinatra (1915-1998) we most often think of the many songs he wrote: "Chicago," "It Was a Very Good Year," and "Strangers in the Night." Possibly his most popular lyric was "My Way." At least, that is what the California media believed, for they played it over and over again on the evening news when they announced his death. The first and last stanzas of "My Way" read:

> And now, the end is near, and so I face the final curtain.
> My friend, I'll say it clear,
> I'll state my case, of which I'm certain.
> I've lived a life that's full, I've traveled each and every highway.
> And more, much more than this,
> I did it my way.
> ....
> For what is a man, what has he got?
> If not himself, then he is naught,
> To say the things, he truly feels,
> And not the words, of one who kneels.
> The record shows, I took the blows—
> And did it my way![1]

---

1. "My Way," co-written by P. Anka and F. Sinatra, 1969.

Though we may prize this kind of rugged self-reliance, yet to boast of doing everything "our way" smacks of pride and arrogance, and as we shall find in this chapter true success comes from doing things God's way. But does this mean that we are locked into a strict pattern of conformity that allows for no freedom of thought or action? The answer is to be found in Joshua 8.

As we reflect on Part II of the Book of Joshua, *viz.*, The Conquest of Central Canaan, 6:1–8:35, we find that after having secured the plain of Jordan the Israelites moved into the highlands. The small town of Ai barred their way. In Joshua 7 we found that the Israelites approached this small city filled with self-confidence over their defeat of Jericho. They were supremely confident of their ability and felt sure they could sweep from their path this seemingly insignificant obstacle. Yet they suffered a humiliating defeat. Now, in chapter 8, we read that they again attacked Ai, and this time their efforts met with success. What separated these two events?

VICTORY OVER AI, 8:1-29

God's Strategy for Taking Ai, 8:1-9.

The sin of Achan and the effect of the defeat of the Israelites by the people of Ai had in all probability weighed heavily on Joshua, leaving him fearful and discouraged. To reassure him the Lord spoke personally to him and said, "Do not fear[2] or be dismayed. Take *all the people of war* with you and arise, go up to Ai; see, I have given into your hand the king of Ai, his people, his city, and his land. You shall do to Ai and its king just as you did to Jericho and its king; you shall take only its spoil and its cattle as plunder for yourselves. Set an ambush for the city behind it" (8:1-2 emphasis added).[3]

There are times in life when we have confessed our sins and fellowship with God has been restored, and yet there is inwardly a feeling of unworthiness that causes us to fear either further failure on our part or God's continued chastening on account of some as yet unconfessed sin. Joshua may have had similar misgivings, and so God spoke to him to encourage him in the present undertaking.

Note that Joshua was told to take "all the people" with him.[4] If we would take these words to heart and mobilize all the church, with each believer using his or her gifts (Ephesians 4:7-12), then we would not be losing the battle against secularism, rationalism, materialism (and all the other isms that are so prevalent today).

Once again, in 8:1, we come across God's use of "I have given"–indicating that the outcome is certain, victory is assured. The city and its people are to be destroyed. Now, however, the spoil may be taken by the men of Israel.

---

2. This exhortation is found throughout the Bible (cf. Joshua 10:8, 25; 11:6; Genesis 15:1; 26:24; Exodus 14:13; 20:20; Numbers 21:34; Jeremiah 1:8; Ezekiel 2:6, as well as in the NT).
3. Cf. Keil, *Joshua*, 84.

To achieve success the Lord instructed Joshua to use a specific strategy.[5] He told Joshua to set men in ambush behind the city--but note that He gave Joshua the freedom to work out the details. In obedience to the word of the Lord, Joshua immediately set about implementing the divine plan. He no longer felt disheartened or discouraged. "So Joshua rose with all the people of war to go up to Ai; and Joshua chose 30,000 men, valiant warriors, and sent them out at night. He commanded them, saying, 'See, you are going to ambush the city from behind it. Do not go very far from the city, but all of you be ready. Then I and all the people who are with me will approach the city. And when they come out

---

4. Considerable confusion exists over the number of men Joshua used in this campaign. Some worthy expositors believe that an error crept into the early manuscripts (cf. Keil, *Joshua*, 86; and M. H. Woudstra, *The Book of Joshua*. New International Commentary on the Old Testament [Grand Rapids: Eerdmans, 1981], 137-38). This is a dangerous expedient as there is no MS evidence to prove it. Others believe that only 30,000 went to attack Ai (e.g., Bush *Genesis*, 88, 90ff.), and that from this number 5,000 were selected to lie in ambush behind the city. Charles C. Ryrie advances the theory that the 30,000 was "a seemingly large number for an ambush." He then goes on to say, "It has been suggested that 'thousand' should read 'chief.' If so, Joshua sent 30 chiefs on a commando-type ambush" (*Ryrie Study Bible, Expanded Edition* [Chicago: Moody, 1995], 343). Still others are of the opinion that the second ambush of 5,000 was really five legions (or about 3,000 men). Cf. The discussions by G. E. Mendenhall, *Journal of Biblical Literature* 77 (1958), 52-66, and G. J. Wenham, *Journal of Biblical Literature* 90 (1971), 142.
5. '*Oreb* is a collective noun and is used of those who comprise the ambush. In 8:9 a different word (*ma'arab*) is used designating the place of the ambush.

to meet us as at the first, we will flee before them. They will come out after us until we have drawn them away from the city, for they will say, "They are fleeing before us as at the first." So we will flee before them. And you shall rise from your ambush and take possession of the city, for Yahweh your God will deliver it into your hand. Then it will be when you have seized the city, that you shall set the city on fire. You shall do it according to the word of Yahweh. See, I have commanded you.' So Joshua sent them away, and they went to the place of ambush and remained between Bethel and Ai, on the west side of Ai; but Joshua spent that night among the people" (8:3-9).[6]

Some might question the wisdom of sending a contingent of men to traverse fifteen miles of rugged terrain at night, but those who have traveled in this part of the world know that the moon is so bright and the sky so clear that visibility at night is more than adequate. Joshua's men could easily have made the journey in the darkness and without detection.

The Success of God's Strategy, 8:10-29.

"Now Joshua rose early in the morning and mustered the people, and he went up with the elders of Israel before the people to Ai. Then all the people of war who were with him went up and drew near and arrived in front of the city, and camped on the north side of Ai. Now there was a valley between him and Ai. And he took about 5,000 men and set

---

6. The issue of the chronology of events has been discussed by W. J. Martin, *Vetus Testament Supplement* 17 (1969), 179-86.

them in ambush between Bethel and Ai, on the west side of the city. So they stationed all the army on the north side of the city, and the rear guard on the west side of the city; and Joshua spent that night in the midst of the valley."

It is possible that the task of this second ambush was to intercept any reinforcements that might come from Bethel.

"It came about when the king of Ai saw it, that the men of the city hurried and rose up early and went out to meet Israel in battle, he and all his people at the appointed place before the desert plain. But he did not know that there was an ambush against him behind the city. Joshua and all Israel pretended to be beaten before them, and fled by the way of the wilderness. And all the people who were in the city were called together to pursue them, and they pursued Joshua and were drawn away from the city. So not a man was left in Ai or Bethel who had not gone out after Israel, and they left the city unguarded and pursued Israel" (8:14-17).

Let us visualize the scene. The king of Ai knew that the Israelites planned to attack Ai again. He also knew that it was unwise to initiate hostilities because of the valley that separated Joshua's forces from his own. He, therefore, waited for the Israelites to make the first move. In the ancient Near East opposing armies might take days, if not weeks preparing for the coming battle. To the king of Ai's surprise he was awakened by his personal bodyguard early the next morning and told of Israel's readiness for battle. He rose quickly and roused his army from their beds. He wanted to attack the Israelites away from the city and not allow Joshua's forces the opportunity to storm the city. In his hasty preparations he had no idea that an ambush had been set behind the city.

When the king of Ai's army came out of the city gates the men of Israel pretended to be beaten and, turning their backs, they ran toward the wilderness. Emboldened by this seemingly easy victory the men of Ai chased after them. No one was left in Ai to defend it. Men from Bethel had apparently come to Ai a day or two before, thus leaving Bethel unprotected.

"Then Yahweh said to Joshua, 'Stretch out the javelin that is in your hand toward Ai, for I will give it into your hand.' So Joshua stretched out the javelin that was in his hand toward the city. The men in ambush rose quickly from their place, and when he had stretched out his hand, they ran and entered the city and captured it, and they quickly set the city on fire. When the men of Ai turned back and looked, behold, the smoke of the city ascended to the sky, and they had no place to flee this way or that, for the people who had been fleeing to the wilderness turned against the pursuers. When Joshua and all Israel saw that the men in ambush had captured the city and that the smoke of the city ascended, they turned back and slew the men of Ai. The others came out from the city to encounter them,[7] so that they were trapped in the midst of Israel, some on this side and some on

---

7. This tacitly implies a greater force than the small number of men in ambush proposed by those who believe the 30,000 is too large. It also corrects the impression that the ambush consisted of about 30 men who waged a guerilla-type of attack.

that side; and the Israelites slew them until no one was left of those who survived or escaped. But they took alive the king of Ai and brought him to Joshua" (8:18-23).

God's plan worked perfectly. At just the right time He told Joshua to give the signal to those lying in ambush. And Joshua, probably standing on some commanding height, did so. The people in ambush quickly rose up, ran through the unguarded city gates, and set the city on fire. On seeing the smoke rising toward the heavens the pursuers naturally desired to return to their city and extinguish the fire. The army with Joshua turned on the men of Ai who were now caught between two powerful forces.

The king of Ai was captured and executed. His body was then hanged on a tree until sundown. It was then thrown into the gate of Ai and a huge heap of stones raised over it (8:29).

No mention is made of conquering Bethel, but in 12:16 Bethel is listed among the cities taken by the Israelites in battle. We may assume, therefore, that a quick attack was made on this small town, and that it fell to Joshua's army without much difficulty. There would also have been plenty of time for such an operation, for "all Israel" left Gilgal and journeyed with their possessions to Shechem where the closing scene of this chapter takes place.

Aftermath of the Battle, 8:30-35

Shechem was approximately 20 miles from Ai and Bethel.[8] It was a very ancient city. The name means a "shoulder, ridge," and this possibly comes from its location. Abraham, on his migration to the land of promise, pitched his tent and built an altar under the oak (or terebinth) of Moreh, at Shechem (Genesis 12:6; Acts 7:16). In John's gospel the city is called Sychar (John 4:5). After Vespasian destroyed the Samaritan temple on Mt. Gerizim, he built his new city ("Neapolis") farther up the valley, leaving ancient Shechem in ruins. Archaeology has shown that ancient Shechem is Tell Balatah (not the site of the later Roman city, which was considered for a long time to be the biblical Shechem). Dr. Arthur P. Stanley calls the location of Shechem "unquestionably ... the most beautiful of all the sites of Western Palestine."[9]

After plundering and burning Ai, Joshua and all Israel made the journey to Shechem to offer sacrifices and give praise to God for His goodness to them. We read: "Then Joshua built an altar to Yahweh, the God of Israel, in Mount Ebal, just as Moses the servant of Yahweh had commanded the sons of Israel, as it is written in the book of the law of Moses, an altar of uncut stones on which no man had

---

8. *Macmillan Bible Atlas,* 44, 46, 55.
9. A. P. Stanley, *Lectures on the History of the Jewish Church*, 3 vols. (London: J. Murray, 1875), 237. Similar comments have been made by the great missionary-traveler-Bible scholar, William M. Thomson, who spent forty-three years as a missionary to the Moslems in Palestine. He wrote his immensely valuable work entitled *The Land and the Book,* 3 vols. (New York: Harper & Brothers, 1886), II:110-12, which I have found tremendously helpful! See also H. B. Tristram, *The Land of Israel: A Journal of Travels in Palestine,* 4th ed. Revised (London: SPCK, 1882), 142-45.

wielded an iron tool; and they offered burnt offerings on it to Yahweh, and sacrificed peace offerings. He wrote there on the stones a copy of the law of Moses, which he had written, in the presence of the sons of Israel. All Israel with their elders and officers and their judges were standing on both sides of the ark before the Levitical priests who carried the ark of the covenant of Yahweh, the stranger as well as the native. Half of them stood in front of Mount Gerizim and half of them in front of Mount Ebal, just as Moses the servant of Yahweh had given command at first to bless the people of Israel. Then afterward he read all the words of the law, the blessing and the curse, according to all that is written in the book of the law. There was not a word of all that Moses had commanded which Joshua did not read before all the assembly of Israel with the women and the little ones and the strangers who were living among them."

But when did the Israelites conquer and take possession of Shechem–the city that guarded the entrance to the valley and was dwarfed on either side by Mounts Ebal and Gerizim?[10]

There is no record of the Israelites ever attacking Shechem, which leaves open the question, How did they come into possession of it? Some believe that the inhabitants of Shechem, when they saw the Israelites marching on their town, surrendered. Others are of the opinion that the Israelites fought with the Shechemites, but that the Bible passes over the attack. Advocates who support this view

---

10. K. A. Kitchen, *Ancient Orient and Old Testament* (Chicago: Inter-Varsity, 1966), 71.

point to chapter 12 and show that other important cities (e.g., Aphek, Taanach, Megiddo) that were situated in the central part of the country were taken without a record being left of how they fell into the hands of the Israelites.[11] Still others claim that because only the Gibeonites made peace with Israel, the people of Shechem may have fled for safety to another, stronger city.

After the Israelites had offered burnt offerings and peace offerings to the Lord, Joshua read to all the people, old and young alike, the words that Moses had inscribed (8:35). He also wrote them on the stones of the altar. Was this the whole Pentateuch (i.e., Genesis through Deuteronomy), or only the Ten Commandments, or was this inscription limited to the blessings and curses of Deuteronomy 28:1-14 and 15-68? The problem remains unresolved.

In conclusion we must admit that this is a sobering passage. Those who believe that "only revelatory" passages of the Bible are inspired are inclined to find fault with some of the specifics and go away from their study unedified. Those who believe in the inerrancy and authority of the Bible are filled with awe as they contemplate the events that are described here, for the apostle Paul wrote: "For whatever was written in earlier times was written for our instruction, so that through perseverance and the encouragement of the Scriptures we might have hope" (Romans 15:4).

---

11. W. G. Dever, *Bulletin of the American Schools of Oriental Research* 216 (1974), 31-52.

CHAPTER 9

THE CONQUEST OF SOUTHERN CANAAN

Part One

JOSHUA 9:1–10:43

The Israelites had learned an important lesson at Ai, and they resolved never again to go into battle without consulting the Lord. They realized that their victory over the people of Jericho had made them vulnerable. They had made the mistake of believing that they were invincible. They had marched on Ai confident of an easy victory. Their initial defeat at Ai had impressed upon them the realization that the Lord was their strength. They realized their weakened position and resolved not to make the same mistake again.

THE TREATY WITH THE GIBEONITES, 9:1-27

The Reaction of the Kings of Southern Canaan to the Defeat of Ai, 9:1-2

Israel's victories over the people of Jericho and Ai had caused the inhabitants of southern Canaan to be filled with fear. To obtain a better understanding of their fears we need to remind ourselves that we experience fear (in the form of anxiety or panic or any number of phobias) when we attribute to a person (or group of people), a place or thing two attributes: The power to do us harm, and the power to take away our freedom. And this was the experience of the Canaanites.

"And it came to pass when all the kings who were on this [the west] side of the Jordan, in the hills and in the lowland and in all the coasts of the Great Sea toward Lebanon--the Hittite, the Amorite, the Canaanite, the Perizzite, the Hivite, and the Jebusite[1]--heard about it [i.e., the defeat of Ai], that they gathered together with one accord to fight with Joshua and Israel."

"But when the inhabitants of Gibeon heard what Joshua had done to Jericho and Ai, they worked craftily, and went and pretended to be ambassadors. And they took old sacks on their donkeys, old wineskins torn and mended, old and patched sandals on their feet, and old garments on themselves; and all the bread of their provision was dry and moldy. And they went to Joshua, to the camp at Gilgal, and said to him and to the men of Israel, 'We have come from a far country; now therefore, make a covenant[2] with us.'"

The Canaanite tribes believed that if they stood together they could defeat the rabble horde that had so recently come

---

1. It is customary to refer to the coalition of the *five* tribes of southern Canaan, yet six are enumerated in 9:1. The explanation is quite simple. The Gibeonites were Hivites and dropped out of the coalition.
2. F. C. Fensham, *Biblical Archaeologist* 27 (1964), 96-100; J. M. Grentz, *Journal of the American Oriental Society* 86 (1966), 113-26.

from the desert. Fear also manifested itself among the Gibeonite confederacy, though in a different way. Initially they agreed to throw in their lot with the other five kings, but secretly decided to first attempt peaceful negotiations through the use subtlety and guile. The word "also" (9:4) does not appear in all translations, but it is in the original text (i.e., "they *also* acted craftily). The Gibeonites agreed in principle to the proposal of the other kings, but decided to secretly use a strategy of their own. If they succeeded, they would be secure and would not need the help of the five kingdoms. If it failed, they could quickly throw in their lot with the royal cities of southern Canaan.

But why did the Gibeonites take such unilateral action? Gibeon was a democracy run by elders. The city-states that proposed the alliance were monarchies, and perhaps the offer of help from the five kings carried with it a conditional element requiring that a king rule Gibeon and Chephirah and Beeroth and Kiriath-jearim (9:17).

The Deception of the Gibeonites, 9:3-15

In the way the Gibeonites approached the Israelites they illustrate the point the Lord Jesus made when He said, "the children of this world are in their generation wiser than the children of light" (Luke 16:8).

Gibeon, known to archaeologists as *Al Jib*,[3] is 8 miles north of Jerusalem and very close to Ai and Bethel. It was a

---

3. Robertson, *Biblical Researches,* I:455-56; Blaikie, *Joshua,* 212-13.

very old city, having been occupied almost continuously from 3100 B.C. to A.D. 325. The elders of Gibeon, when they received word of the defeat of Ai, thought only of their people. The kings of the five cities were inclined to think first of themselves (note the emphasis on "me" in 10:4). Though an alliance may have given them added strength, in the long run it may have proved detrimental to their way of life.

When the leaders of Gibeon heard what Joshua had done to Jericho and to Ai, they acted "with one mouth." They decided to send an envoy to try to seduce the Israelites into entering into a covenant with them. There was legislation permitting the Israelites to make peace with more distant people, but not with the people of Canaan (Deuteronomy 20:10-15). To add a touch of visual realism to their entreaty and graphically portray the long distance they had supposedly traveled, they took worn-out sacks on their donkeys, and wineskins worn-out and torn and mended, and worn-out and patched sandals on their feet, and worn-out clothes on their backs; and dry and crumbled bread in their bags. And they came to Joshua at Gilgal and said to him and to the men of Israel, "We have come from a far country; now therefore, make a covenant with us" (9:3-6).

Their craftiness is seen in different ways. Nothing was left to chance. Though realizing that the hand of God was against them, yet, instead of repenting and humbling themselves before Him, they sought to thwart God by duping His servants. And, as we shall see, they were successful ... but only up to a point.

When the delegation from Gibeon arrived at Gilgal, "The men of Israel said to the Hivites, 'Perhaps you are living within our land; how then shall we make a covenant with you?'" But the Gibeonites obliquely sidestepped the thrust of this question and addressing Joshua, said: "We are your servants" (in other words, we mean you no harm). Then Joshua said to them, "Who are you and where do you come from?" This time the Gibeonites parried the direct thrust of Joshua's question by using flattery and pretending to be devout seekers after he truth. They said to Joshua, "Your servants have come from a very far country because of the fame of Yahweh your God; for we have heard the report of Him and all that He did in Egypt, and all that He did to the two kings of the Amorites who were beyond the Jordan, to Sihon king of Heshbon and to Og king of Bashan who was at Ashtaroth. So our elders and all the inhabitants of our country spoke to us, saying, 'Take provisions in your hand for the journey, and go to meet them and say to them, "We are your servants; now then, make a covenant with us."' This our bread was warm when we took it for our provisions out of our houses on the day that we left to come to you; but now behold, it is dry and has become crumbled. These wineskins which we filled were new, and behold, they are torn; and these our clothes and our sandals are worn out because of the very long journey."

"So the men of Israel took some of their provisions, and did not ask for the counsel of Yahweh. And Joshua made peace with them and made a covenant with them, to let them live; and the leaders of the congregation swore an oath to them."

The cunning lies and deception of the Gibeonites are easy for us to recognize. Joshua, however, did not have the benefit of hindsight. We note their feigned sincerity, "We have come from a far country" (9:6); then their desire to be in a covenant relationship with God's people ("make a covenant with us" mentioned prominently throughout) (9:6); their supposed willingness to be subservient to Israel, "we are your servants" (9:8, etc.); and their flattery, "we have come from a very far country *because of the fame of Yahweh your God*" (9:9).

They cunningly sidestepped Joshua's questions, "Who are you, and where do you come from?" and instead recounted their knowledge of Israel's victories over Bashan and Og; They wisely left out the recent victories over the people of Jericho and Ai, for if they were from a distant land how could they be expected to know of these recent events. Then to convince Joshua and the elders of Israel they presented their "evidence"–worn-out clothing and wineskins, and moldy food. The Israelites believed what they saw and were completely taken in by these skillful liars. And "Joshua made peace with them and made a covenant with them, to let them live; and the leaders of the congregation swore an oath to them" (9:15).

It is easy for us to blame Joshua and the elders of Israel for not seeking the mind of the Lord, but before we do so let us consider how often we have been swayed by the evidence of our senses. To this Dr. George Bush utters a timely word of caution: The "pretense [of the Gibeonites] was well calculated to prevail with the Israelites, for those who are guileless themselves are least suspicious of guile in others, and nothing wins more upon the simple-heartedness of good people than the appearance of piety and devotion ... where it was not expected."[4]

The biblical writer then adds a postscript to the day's proceedings, "So the men of Israel ... did not ask for the counsel of the Lord." They could have consulted the Urim and Thummim, but they were unaccustomed to doing so. At a later time David used these instruments quite often, but at this early period of Israel's history, seeking to know God's will by this means was seldom though done.

People today may excuse themselves from seeking to know God's leading because we no longer have these mystic elements that were a part of Israel's religion. That is true, but we do have God's Word and the inner witness of the Holy Spirit, and as we spend time each and every day meditating on some portion of it, and observe to do all that is written in it, we enjoy good success. Furthermore we are told that it is as a result of the *use* we make of Scripture that our senses will be trained to discern good and evil (Hebrews 5:13-14).

The Punishment of the Gibeonites, 9:16-27

The Gibeonites probably returned to Gibeon congratulating themselves on their success. Their elation, however, was short-lived. "'A lying tongue is but for a moment.' and the Gibeonite fraud lived for just three days. Then it was discovered by Joshua that the Gibeonites lived in the imme-

---

4. Bush, *Joshua*, 104.

diate neighborhood.... Nothing could have been more provoking than to discover that he and the elders had been duped. It is always a bitter experience to find that our confidence has been misplaced. Before all the inhabitants of Canaan he and his people had been humiliated. Not a man in all the country but would be making merry at their expense."[5]

Once the sons of Israel learned the truth about their treaty with the Gibeonites, they "set out and came to their cities on the third day. Now their cities were Gibeon and Chephirah and Beeroth and Kiriath-jearim... And the whole congregation grumbled against the leaders. But all the leaders said to the whole congregation, 'We have sworn to them by Yahweh, the God of Israel, and now we cannot touch them. This we will do to them, even let them live, so that wrath will not be upon us for the oath which we swore to them...'"

"Then Joshua called for them and spoke to them, saying, 'Why have you deceived us, saying, "We are very far from you," when you are living within our land? Now therefore, you are cursed, and you shall never cease being slaves, both hewers of wood and drawers of water for the house of my God.' So they answered Joshua and said, 'Because it was certainly told your servants that Yahweh your God had commanded His servant Moses to give you all the land, and to destroy all the inhabitants of the land before you; therefore we feared greatly for our lives because of you, and have done this thing. Now behold, we are in your

---

5. Blaikie, *Joshua*, 216.

hands; do as it seems good and right in your sight to do to us.'"

The Result of Wrongful Actions. "Thus [Joshua] did to them, and delivered them from the hands of the sons of Israel, and they did not kill them. But Joshua made them that day hewers of wood and drawers of water[6] for the congregation and for the altar of Yahweh, to this day, in the place which He would choose."

It has been argued that inasmuch as the Gibeonites were not truthful, the covenant Joshua and the elders of Israel made with them could be set aside. And certainly if this was merely a human contract that would be apropos, but this one had been sworn in the name of the Lord, and He is above such actions. The punishment inflicted by the Israelites was sufficient, and the Gibeonites acknowledged the justness of the sentence.

The Gibeonites gained the ends they sought, but in three days their fraud was discovered. The suzerainty-vassal treaty they had gained was suddenly changed, and they and each succeeding generation had a lifetime to live with the consequences.

This emphasizes the fact that we must live with the consequences of our wrongful actions. This truth is self-evident, but people today do all they can to circumvent the teaching of God's Word. Take for example the numerous

---

6. This was "hard labor" from which there would be no relief (see Thomson, *The Land and the Book*, I:57, 118).

cases of out-of-wedlock pregnancies. Whatever choice is made, the couple has to live with the consequences of their actions. And the same is true of marriage to an unbeliever (Mark 10:11-12; 1 Corinthians 7:10-11). Scripture, however, is inclusive of other sins: "Do you not know that the unrighteous will not inherit the kingdom of God? Do not be deceived; neither fornicators, nor idolaters, nor adulterers, nor effeminate, nor homosexuals, nor thieves, nor the covetous, nor drunkards, nor revilers, nor swindlers, will inherit the kingdom of God" (1 Corinthians 6:10-11). Those who practice such things must be prepared to live with the consequences.

The Importance of Our Vows. The treaty with the Gibeonites remained in effect until the time of King Saul (2 Samuel 21:1-14). At a time when his sagging popularity reached an all-time low, he wanted to impress the people with his zeal for the Lord. He killed the Gibeonites (so that he could give their lands to his officers). For years, God allowed this violation of the covenant to go unpunished. During David's reign, however, it was redressed.

Some preachers encourage young people to make vows. These may take the form of surrendering oneself to a lifetime of missionary service, or giving money to some worthy cause, or abstaining from some desirable practice so as to devote one's time to prayer or some form of Christian service. The covenants we make with the Lord are important, and we should not treat them lightly. If we are unable to fulfill them then we should earnestly seek God's forgiveness. Otherwise we need to do all we can to perform our promise (Ecclesiastes 5:4-5).

The Way to Overcome Our Fears. While fear had driven the Gibeonites to deceive the Israelites (9:24), yet that same fear also made them willing to submit themselves to the penalty imposed by Joshua and the elders (9:25). And throughout their generations they were loyal to the decision they had made. Being hewers of wood and carriers of water also brought them into contact with the Levitical priesthood and the Temple where the true God was worshiped. With hearts opened toward the Lord (as Rahab's was) we trust that many came to saving faith.[7]

We, too, have to face our fears, and the way to resolve them is to submit ourselves to the Lord and trust in His sovereign goodwill toward us (Romans 8:38-39; cf. Luke 12:4). I like Dr. Charles Ryrie's footnote to Psalm 46:1-3, "A *refuge* provides shelter from danger. *Strength* gives us courage in danger. *Very present help* can also have the idea of 'well-proved help.' God's help is both present and proven, ready and reliable."

These are practical truths we should not forget.

---

7. Cf. Schaeffer, *Joshua and the Flow of Biblical History*, 149-51.

CHAPTER 10

THE CONQUEST OF SOUTHERN CANAAN

Part Two

JOSHUA 10:1-43

Some years ago, while teaching a course on the life of Christ, I found to my chagrin that my students remembered an illustration I gave but forgot the point I was making. I had asked why Judas accepted so little money from the priests (i.e., only "thirty shekels of silver") when he agreed to betray Christ to them? (cf. Zechariah 11:12-13; see also Exodus 21:32). To illustrate the point that "thirty shekels of silver" had become an expression for something of trifling worth, I referred to the Sumerian poem, "The Curse of Agade."

The Sumerian king, Sargon the Great, was known for his political accomplishments as well as his building projects. The city of Agade was his most enterprising project. After several years of occupation, Sargon (so the story goes) angered the gods of the Sumerian pantheon and a curse was placed on Agade. It was to fall into ruin, and eventually no one would live there.

Some years after Sargon's death another king was engaged in conquests in the area. When he passed by Agade, it appeared to him to be so disreputable he exclaimed that it wasn't worth "thirty shekels of silver" (i.e., not worth the effort of ransacking the place). From this we realize that "thirty shekels of silver" had become a colloquial expression for something of insignificant value[1].

To my chagrin, my students remembered the illustration, but forgot the point I was making.

It is much the same with Joshua 10. The emphasis of the passage is on the victories of God as a Warrior and the conquests He gave His people. Verses 12 and 13 describe what has come to be known as "Joshua's Long Day." Readers of the story invariably remember Joshua's command--
" 'Sun, stand still over Gibeon;
And Moon, in the Valley of Aijalon.'
So the sun stood still,
And the moon stopped,
Till the people had taken revenge
Upon their enemies"--
but they have only a hazy recollection of the reason for his command. Realizing how easy it is for people to become absorbed in a facet of the story and miss the "big picture," I shall deal only briefly with verses 12 and 13.

---

1. S. N. Kramer, *The Sumerians: Their History, Culture, and Character* (Chicago: U. of Chicago Press, 1963), 59-66.

THE DESTRUCTION OF THE AMORITE COALITION, 10:1-43

The Consternation of the Amorite King, 10:1-2

"Now it came about when Adoni-zedek king of Jerusalem heard that Joshua had captured Ai, and had utterly destroyed it (just as he had done to Jericho and its king, so he had done to Ai and its king), and that the inhabitants of Gibeon had made peace with Israel and were within their land, that he feared greatly, because Gibeon was a great city, like one of the royal cities, and because it was greater than Ai, and all its men were mighty."

Adoni-zedek, whose name means "lord of righteousness," was king of Jerusalem.[2] Earlier (around 2085 B.C.), when Abraham had returned from the slaughter of the kings of the East (Genesis 14), he met a man named Melchizedek (meaning "king of righteousness") who was king in Salem (Jerusalem). The difference in the meaning of their names is very slight, leading us to believe that "Adoni-zedek" may have become a titular title like "Pharaoh" in Egypt. Whereas Melchizedek was an honorable man and priest of the Most High God, it is doubtful that Adoni-zedek lived up to his name for his actions indicate that he was concerned about himself and not his people (cf. Joshua 11:19).

When Adoni-zedek learned that the neighboring city of Gibeon[3] had made a covenant with Joshua he became very

---

2. This is the first time the name "Jerusalem" is used in the Bible. Its earlier name was "Salem," meaning "peace."

afraid. Word had spread of how the Israelites were engaged in a war to purge all Amorites and Canaanites from the land, and the fate that had overtaken Jericho and Ai gave them good cause for alarm. But what should Adoni-zedek do? Gibeon was a great city, comparable in size and strength to one of the "royal" cities. And Gibeon was only six miles from Jerusalem.

The Coalition of the Southern Kingdoms, 10:3-7

In light of his fears "Adoni-zedek king of Jerusalem sent to Hoham king of Hebron, Piram king of Jarmuth, Japhia king of Lachish, and Debir king of Eglon, saying, 'Come up to me and help me, that we may attack Gibeon, for it has made peace with Joshua and with the children of Israel.' "

"Therefore the five kings of the Amorites, the king of Jerusalem, the king of Hebron, the king of Jarmuth, the king of Lachish, and the king of Eglon, gathered together and went up, they and all their armies, and camped before Gibeon and made war against it. And the men of Gibeon sent to Joshua at the camp at Gilgal, saying, 'Do not forsake your servants; come up to us quickly, save us and help us, for all the kings of the Amorites who dwell in the mountains have gathered together against us.' So Joshua ascended

---

3. J. B. Pritchard, *Vetus Testamentum* Supplement 7 (1960), 4-5, 11-12. Cf., M. Avi-Yonah, ed., *Encyclopedia of Archaeological Excavations in the Holy Land* (1976), II:446-50.

from Gilgal, he and all the people of war with him, and all the mighty men of valor."

Jerusalem may have been *the* leading city of the southern confederation of "city-states." To allay his fears Adonizedek sent messages to the other kings of the Amorites requesting that they join forces with him in attacking Gibeon. They readily agreed, and their combined forces encircled Gibeon.

The Gibeonites probably sent word to Joshua as soon as they saw the armies of the southern coalition gathering somewhere north of Jerusalem to make war on their city. This messenger hastened to Gilgal approximately thirty miles away to the place where Joshua and the Israelites had their base of operations.

When word of the plight of the Gibeonites was disseminated through the camp of Israel there may have been some who believed that no help should be given them inasmuch as the covenant that had been made with them was the result of lies and misrepresentation. If so, then the leaders of Israel felt differently. They certainly did not want to take on the five kings of the Amorites, but realized that they had an obligation to do so. They had given their word in the name of the Lord, and they could not go back on their vow.

In the help given the Gibeonites we find encouragement for us in our Christian lives. When we pray earnestly to the Lord, He hears us and sends us the help we need.

The Encouragement of the Lord, 10:8

By way of encouraging Joshua the Lord said to him, "Do not fear them [i.e., the coalition], for I have given them into your hands; not one of them shall stand before you."[4] Once again the outcome was assured, and Joshua was promised that the potential difficulties would, in reality, be a blessing in disguise.

The Intervention of the Lord, 10:9-14

"So Joshua came upon them suddenly by marching all night from Gilgal.[5] And Yahweh confounded them before Israel, and He slew them with a great slaughter at Gibeon, and pursued them by the way of the ascent of Beth-horon and struck them as far as Azekah and Makkedah. As they fled from before Israel, while they were at the descent of Beth-horon, Yahweh threw large stones from heaven on them as far as Azekah, and they died; there were more who died from the hailstones than those whom the sons of Israel killed with the sword.[6]

"At that time Joshua spoke to Yahweh when Yahweh delivered up the Amorites before the sons of Israel, and he said in the sight of Israel,

---

4. See P. D. Miller, *The Divine Warrior in Early Israel* (Cambridge, MA: Harvard U. P., 1973), 123-28; G. H. Jones, *Vetus Testamentum* 25 (1975), 653-55.
5. Thomson, *The Land and the Book*, I:357-58.
6. *Macmillan Bible Atlas*, 34, 56.

'O sun, stand still at Gibeon,
And O moon in the valley of Aijalon.'
So the sun stood still, and the moon stopped,
Until the nation avenged themselves of their enemies.' "

"Is it not written in the book of Jashar? And the sun stopped in the middle of the sky and did not hasten to go down for about a whole day. There was no day like that before it or after it, when Yahweh listened to the voice of a man; for Yahweh fought for Israel."[7]

The army of Israel had traveled approximately thirty miles from Gilgal to Gibeon in central Canaan. They had probably arrived shortly before dawn. At Joshua's command the Israelites launched a sudden, surprise attack, catching the Amorite coalition off guard. The Lord gave Israel a great victory, and He[8] killed a significant number of their enemies at Gibeon. The Amorites were routed and took off in different directions as fast as their legs could carry them. Initially some made for Beth-horon,[9] and here the Lord cast great hailstones on the fleeing coalition,[10] and

---

7. T. Smith, *The History of Joshua*, 148f., has an excellent discussion of the content and "value" of the Book of Jasher.
8. The original text reads "He," whereas we would have expected "they." While the Israelites did the killing, it was the Lord who gave them the victory. The use of "He" shows God's close identification with His people.
9. J. G. Geikie, *The Holy Land and the Bible*, 2 vols. (New York: Cassell, 1887), II:181-82; and Robinson, *Biblical Researches*, II:251-55.

killed more of them than had perished at the hand of the Israelites. Others fled northwest toward Azekah, while still others ran toward Makkedah, fourteen miles southwest of Jerusalem.

With verses 12-14 we come across a difficult interpretative problem. Did the earth actually stop its rotation around the sun or was there some refraction of the sun's light that prolonged daylight and enabled the Israelites to continue fighting?[11] Is the language poetic or does the text merely describe an eclipse of the sun giving the appearance of a lengthened day when the sun reappeared from behind the moon? Scholars line up on all sides of these issues with most doubting the literal meaning of the text because of the cataclysmic consequences (tidal waves, a change in the seasons of the year, temperature increase that could wipe out all life, etc.) to the earth if its rotation around the sun was suspended. *But let us remember that the Members of the Trinity who brought worlds into existence by with a word (cf. Psalm 33:6-9) could most assuredly sustain the world in a situation that might otherwise destroy it (note Colossians 1:17; Hebrews 1:3). Though many have quibbled about verse 12, verse 13 certainly implies such an occurrence.*[12]

Those who reject this view invariably hold to a uniformitarian approach to all reality that makes no allowance for a temporary change in the order of the universe. They point

---

10. Josephus, *Antiquities of the Jews*, V:1:58-61. See also The Apocrypha, *Ecclesiasticus*, 46:6.
11. Josephus, *Antiquities of the Jews,* V:1:17.

to the word *dom*, "stand still, be silent," and inform us that an eclipse took place so that the sun was concealed.[13] This was supposedly very beneficial, for during the eclipse the sun did not pour down its heat on the already tired Israeli soldiers. Still others believe Joshua's words of command to the moon were for an astrological sign.[14] And then there are those who believe that these verses are poetic because reference is made to the Book of Jasher *(Sepher hayashar*, "Book of the Upright"), which is believed to be a collection of poems or national ballads celebrating chief events in the wars of Israel. No copy is extant through some Jewish rabbis claim to have seen it.

Whichever view is adopted, daytime was prolonged so that the Israelites could achieve a great victory over their enemies.

---

12. For a detailed explanation of what might have happened, see H. Rimmer, *The Harmony of Science and Scripture* (Grand Rapids: Eerdmans, 1936), 251-83. Other views are treated in J. Blenkinsopp, *Gibeon and Israel* (Cambridge: Cambridge U. P., 1972), 41-52; M. J. Gruenthaner, *Catholic Biblical Quarterly* 10 (1948), 271-90; J. S. Holladay, *Journal of Biblical literature* 87 (1968), 166-78.
13. R. D. Wilson, *Princeton Theological Review* 16 (1918), 46-54; W. C. Kaiser, Jr., *Hard Sayings of the Old Testament* (Downers Grove, IL: InterVarsity, 1992), 123-26.
14. J. S. Holladay, Jr., *Journal of Biblical Literature* 87 (1968), 166-78.

The Capture of the Amorite Kings, 10:16-27

"Now the five kings [of the Amorites] had fled and hidden themselves in a cave at Makkedah. And it was told Joshua, saying, 'The five kings have been found hidden in the cave at Makkedah.' So Joshua said, 'Roll large stones against the mouth of the cave, and set men by it to guard them. And do not stay there yourselves, but pursue your enemies, and attack their rear guard. Do not allow them to enter their cities, for Yahweh your God has delivered them into your hand.' Then it happened, while Joshua and the children of Israel made an end of slaying them (i.e., the Amorites) with a very great slaughter, till they had finished, that those who escaped entered fortified cities. And all the people returned to the camp, to Joshua at Makkedah, in peace. No one moved his tongue against any of the children of Israel" (10:16-21).

Someone had seen the five Amorite kings hiding in the cave near the town of Makkedah, and they related this news to Joshua. He, wisely, had them "imprison" the kings there while his men continued their pursuit of the enemy. When they had achieved a great victory, they returned to Joshua.

"Then Joshua said, 'Open the mouth of the cave, and bring out those five kings to me from the cave.' And they did so ... So it was, when they brought out those kings to Joshua, that Joshua called for all the men of Israel, and said to the captains of the men of war who went with him, 'Come near, put your feet on the necks of these kings.' And they drew near and put their feet on their necks. Then Joshua said to them, 'Do not be afraid, nor be dismayed; be strong and of good courage, for this is what Yahweh will do to all your enemies against whom you fight.' And afterward Joshua struck them and killed them, and hanged them on five trees; and they were hanging on the trees until evening. So it was at the time of the going down of the sun that Joshua commanded, and they took them down from the trees, cast them into the cave where they had hidden, and laid large stones against the cave's mouth, which remain until this very day" (10:22-27).

There are some Bible scholars, however, who are inclined to interpret the biblical text in light of current social mores, and neglect to take into consideration either the social customs of Joshua's times or the command of the Lord. They feel that clemency should have been extended to the five Amorite kings, and having the captains of the men of war place their feet on the necks of their enemies was degrading to these monarchs for whom defeat was sufficient humiliation. It should be pointed out that the placing one's foot on the neck of a defeated enemy was a common practice in those days, and having the captains participate in this drama served to assure them and their men of future victories.

Verse 21 should also be taken seriously by Joshua's critics. No one living at that time spoke ill of his actions.

The Decisive Nature of the Conquest, 10:28-39

"That day [i.e., At that time] Joshua captured Makkedah, and struck it and its king with the edge of the sword; he utterly destroyed it and every person who was in it. He left no survivor. Thus he did to the king of Makkedah just as he had done to the king of Jericho. Then Joshua and all Israel with him passed on from Makkedah to Libnah, and fought against Libnah. Yahweh gave it also with its king into the hands of Israel, and he struck it and every person who was in it with the edge of the sword. He left no survivor in it. Thus he did to its king just as he had done to the king of Jericho. And Joshua and all Israel with him passed on from Libnah to Lachish ... Then Horam king of Gezer came up to help Lachish, and Joshua defeated him and his people until he had left him no survivor. And Joshua and all Israel with him passed on from Lachish to Eglon, and they camped by it and fought against it. They captured it on that day and struck it with the edge of the sword; and he utterly destroyed that day every person who was in it.... Then Joshua and all Israel with him went up from Eglon to Hebron, and they fought against it. They captured it and struck it and its king and all its cities and all the persons who were in it with the edge of the sword. He left no survivor .... Then Joshua and all Israel with him returned to Debir, and they fought against it. He captured it and its king and all its cities, and they struck them with the edge of the sword, and utterly destroyed every person who was in it. He left no survivor. Just as he had done to Hebron, so he did to Debir and its king...."

Joshua's conquest was rapid. He passed from one city to another in rapid succession. It is evident that after their fall none of these cities were garrisoned with Israelis. That is why after Hebron had been captured, when Joshua's army withdrew, Canaanites came and inhabited the city. This made it necessary for Caleb to conquer Hebron again (14:6-15).

Summary, 10:40-43

"So Joshua subdued the whole region, including the hill country, the Negev, the western foothills and the mountain slopes, together with all their kings. He left no survivors. He totally destroyed all who breathed, just as Yahweh, the God of Israel, had commanded. Joshua subdued them from Kadesh-Barnea to Gaza and from the whole region of Goshen to Gibeon. All these kings and their lands Joshua conquered in one campaign, because Yahweh, the God of Israel, fought for Israel. Then Joshua returned with all Israel to the camp at Gilgal."

Joshua had probably received the news of the southern coalition of "city-states" with misgiving. It was one thing to take on one city at a time, but five powerful ones all at once was daunting. The Lord nevertheless spoke to reassure Joshua, and in faith Joshua made the night journey to relieve the siege of Gibeon. And not only did the Lord give Joshua the victory over the five kings, but the entire area capitulated before his army. More was accomplished in this short span of time (note 10:42, "at one stroke, at one time"), leaving Joshua free to concentrate on the northern kingdoms.

But many Occidentals are upset at the thought of the Lord of glory desiring the massacre of all living beings in Canaan. To them the thought of Yahweh as a warrior is abhorrent. And when Numbers 31 is factored into their thinking it is easier for them to follow the teaching of liberal theologians and conclude that the God of the Old Testament is harsh and bloodthirsty, and only in the New Testament do we read of a God of love and grace. Such thinking develops a mind set that unwittingly concludes that only that which we approve is right. Those who reason this way forget that the Lord our God is sovereign, and the Old Testament merely prepares us for the events of the Book of Revelation when God's wrath will be poured out on all His enemies.

Of practical value is the fact that the Lord sometimes brings us face to face with seemingly insurmountable odds (as He did with Joshua and the Israelites) in order to reveal His power. And though at the present time our armies are engaged in warfare far from our shores, yet we struggle against ungodly rulers, secular powers, the world forces of this darkness, the spiritual forces of wickedness in the heavenly places (cf. Ephesians 6:12). The assurance God gave Joshua is therefore of great encouragement to us (Matthew 28:20).

CHAPTER 11

THE CONQUEST OF NORTHERN CANAAN

JOSHUA 11:1–12:24

When my sons were much younger, they would go downstairs on Saturday mornings and watch cartoons on television. Among their favorites was "Tom and Jerry," the famous cat and mouse duo. My sociology teacher had told those of us in his class the reason why kids supposedly loved the escapades of this couple. The cat, Tom, was supposed to represent a child's parents who made his or her life miserable, and the mouse, Jerry, was of course the child who was constantly being thwarted in his or her desire to have fun.

One Saturday morning I decided to watch some of the cartoons with my sons. (Needless to say I was chagrined at the thought that sociologists cast me and others like me in a sadistic roll in which a parent supposedly delighted in tormenting his children!) The cartoon I watched showed Tom chasing Jerry through the house. Jerry, of course, escaped (just in time) through a small hole in a skirting board, and Tom tried vainly to catch Jerry by sticking his paw into the hole and trying to snag Jerry with his claws.

Not to be outdone by his persecutor, Jerry obtained a blowtorch which he dragged across the floor and positioned close to Tom's exposed posterior. Jerry then lit the blowtorch and watched as Tom rear turned from pink to red hot.

All of a sudden the pain registered and Tom let out a yell that was accompanied by him becoming airborne. He found relief by soaking his rear end in the fishpond in the front yard.

Naturally my sons laughed hysterically. I, however, did not find in this cartoon a description of a child wanting to get even with a heartless parent. What I saw was a portrayal of an *externally oriented* person–someone who was oblivious to the needs of others and did not make decisions until he or she was forced to do so. As we shall see, Joshua serves as a good example of someone who is *internally oriented*, took the initiative, set goals, and worked toward achieving them.

CONQUERING THE LAND OF CANAAN, 6:1–12:24, continued.

We have been working our way through the book of Joshua, and have taken note of:
> The Entrance of the Israelites into the land of Canaan, 1:1–5:15, and
> The Conquest of the Land God had Promised to Give His People (6:1–12:24).

We also found that 6:1–12:24 can be divided neatly into three parts:
> The Conquest of Central Canaan, 6:1–8:35,
> The Conquest of Southern Canaan, 9:1–10:43, and
> The Conquest of Northern Canaan, 11:1-15.

This is followed by a summary of the conquests, 11:16–12:24.

The Conquest of Northern Canaan, 11:1-15

These verses may be divided into four sections that are clearly discernable. When Jabin, king of Hazor heard of the destruction of the southern coalition of Amorite city-states, he determined to call together his allies. He hoped that together they could confront the Israelites and put an end to their occupation of Canaan.

The Northern Alliance. "Jabin" was probably a hereditary title like Ben-Hadad in Syria or Pharaoh in Egypt.[1] The name means "one who is intelligent," or "discerning." The city from which Jabin ruled was located nine miles north of the Sea of Galilee at Tell el-Qedah. It was the largest city in Palestine in Old Testament times, and reached its peak in the fifteenth to fourteenth centuries B.C. Archaeologists have estimated that it may have had a population of 40,000. The city itself was divided into two parts. It consisted of a bottle-shaped mound about 130 feet high with the upper city covering 25 to 30 acres. The lower city occupied between 175 to 200 acres, and was massive when compared to Jericho (about five acres) and Megiddo (approximately 20 acres). Jabin was a powerful monarch, and it is easy to see how he exerted great influence on the city-states of northern Canaan.

---

1. See Y. Yadin, *Hazor* (London: Oxford U. P., 1972), 5-6; Boling and Wright, *Joshua*, 304.

As a part of Jabin's plan for self-preservation he "sent to Jobab king of Madon, to the king of Shimron, to the king of Achshaph, [2] and to the kings who were from the north, in the mountains, in the plain south of Chinneroth, in the lowland, and in the heights of Dor on the west, to the Canaanites in the east and in the west, [even to] the Amorite, the Hittite, the Perizzite, the Jebusite in the mountains, and the Hivite below Hermon in the land of Mizpah." These kings and their armies joined forces with Jabin and were so many that they resembled "the sand that is on the seashore in multitude, with very many horses and chariots." They met and camped at the waters of Merom.

This was a formidable alliance. Initially it was comprised of Canaanites, but Jabin expanded the scope beyond the two kings who had probably signed treaties with him, to include other ethnic groups. According to Josephus their combined strength was 300,000 armed foot soldiers, 10,000 cavalrymen, and 20,000 chariots.[3] It is possible that their goal was to march down the Jordan River valley and attack the people of Israel on the open plain before the ruins of Jericho.

As soon as Joshua learned of this alliance, he took immediate action. He was proactive. Summoning all his men, he traveled north as fast as possible.

---

2. C. Rasmussen, *NIV Atlas of the Bible* (Grand Rapids: Zondervan, 1989), 95.
3. Josephus, *Antiquities of the Jews,* V:1:18. His figures cannot be corroborated.

God's Timely Encouragement, 11:6-9. Even though the force to be encountered was vast so that the Canaanites and their allies filled the valley where they had pitched their tents, there was no dramatic or miraculous intervention by the Lord this time. Instead He encouraged Joshua with the words, "Do not be afraid because of them, for tomorrow[4] at this time I will deliver all of them slain before Israel."

That was all, but it was enough? Yes. If we paraphrase God's promise, it would run something like this: "You see their vast numbers? Don't be afraid of them. Before the sun sets tomorrow evening they'll all be dead." "So Joshua and all the people of war with him came upon them suddenly by the waters of Merom, and attacked them, and Yahweh gave them into the hand of Israel who defeated them and pursued them all the way to Greater Sidon, to Misrephoth Maim, and to the Valley of Mizpeh on the east. No survivors were left."

We would love to know the details of the battle, but none are given apart from Israel's surprise attack. We are left to imagine the bewilderment of the Canaanite alliance, the panic that ensued, and their flight (*mippene*, "from the face") from before the army of Israel. Sidon was to the west, on the Mediterranean coast; Misrephoth Maim was

---

4. Joshua and the army of Israel must have been very close to the waters of Merom for the Lord to promise victory the next day, for Merom was upwards of 70 miles from Gilgal. We are justified in concluding that when information of the alliance of Canaanites reached Joshua, and before the Lord spoke to reassure him, Joshua had already marched north with all his men of war.

probably along the Litani River; and the Valley of Mizpeh was to the east. The rout of the Canaanite alliance was complete, and no survivors were left.

Once again the victory given the Israelites reveals the Lord of glory to be a "warrior" (Exodus 15:3), who knows how to make war and possesses the power to destroy His enemies.

And Joshua did all that the Lord had commanded him (11:6). He hamstrung their horses, thus rendering them unfit for battle. He also burned the Canaanites' chariots. In this way the temptation for Israel to use these things in future battles was removed. The Lord was their surest defense, and as long as their eyes were on Him, and they lived in obedience to His revealed will, He would give them success.

Israel's Complete Victory, 11:10-13. After completing the destruction of the northern tribes, Joshua returned and "and captured Hazor and killed its king with the sword; for Hazor formerly was the head of all these kingdoms. They also killed every person who was in it with the edge of the sword, utterly destroying them; there was no one left who breathed. And he burned Hazor with fire[5]. Joshua captured all the cities of these kings, and all their kings, and he killed them with the edge of the sword, and utterly destroyed them; just as Moses the servant of Yahweh had

---

5. B. K. Waltke, *Bibliotheca Sacra* 129 (1972), 33-47. Cf. M. Avi-Yonah, ed., *Encyclopedia of Archaeological Excavations in the Holy Land* (1976), II:474-95.

commanded. However, Israel did not burn any cities that stood on their mounds, except Hazor alone .... Just as Yahweh had commanded Moses His servant, so Moses commanded Joshua, and so Joshua did; *he left nothing undone of all that Yahweh had commanded Moses*"[6] (emphasis added).

Only Hazor was burned. The other cities were left intact, so that the Israelites would be able to inherit "large, flourishing cities that they did not build, houses filled with all kinds of good things that they did not provide, wells that they did not dig, and vineyards and olive groves that they did not plant" (cf. Deuteronomy 6:10-11).

The Division of the Spoils of War, 11:14-15. "And all the spoil of these cities and the livestock, the children of Israel took as booty for themselves; but they struck every man with the edge of the sword until they had destroyed them, and they left none breathing. As Yahweh had commanded Moses his servant, so Moses commanded Joshua, and so Joshua did. He left nothing undone of all that Yahweh had commanded Moses."

Israel's spoils must have been great by this time, and to have borne tacit witness to the faithfulness of Joshua to all that Moses had taught. His faithfulness forms a kind of benchmark to which other leaders should strive to attain.

---

6. What a remarkable testimony!

Summary of the Conquest, 11:16–12:24.

The verses contained in this section of the book of Joshua can be likened to a travelog such as is seen at the beginning of documentaries of the National Geographic Society or programs on the Discovery or History channels. These programs often begin with an overview–an eagle's eye view over the terrain in which the events took place–and this sets the stage for what is to follow. It is excellent pedagogical methodology!

Introduction, 11:16-23. These verses provide an overview of what Joshua and the men of Israel accomplished. They begin in the south and move northward. The Negev or southland is a term that refers to the little-watered region situated south of Judea. In Bible times it was a principal grazing area. It covers about 3,600 square miles and contains important biblical sites such as Kadesh-Barnea and Beer-sheba.[7] The Arabah is a word generally applied to a desert area, but specifically refers to the valley between the Dead Sea and the Gulf of Aqaba. The valley is about one hundred miles in length and is somewhat wider in the north than in the south.

Mount Halak is unknown, but its proximity to Mount Seir (Easu's fortress, also known as Petra) pinpoints its general location. The northern point of Joshua's conquests

---

7. Cf. N. Glueck, *Rivers in the Desert: A History of the Negev* (New York: Grove, 1959), 302pp. See also Glueck, *The Biblical Archaeologist* 22 no.4 (1959): 82-97.

extended all the way to Baal Gad (unknown) and the foot of Mount Hermon in the north.[8]

"Joshua made war a long time with all those kings. There was not a city that made peace with the children of Israel, except the Hivites, the inhabitants of Gibeon. All the others they took in battle. For it was Yahweh's intent to harden their hearts, that they should come against Israel in battle, that He might utterly destroy them, and that they might receive no mercy, but that He might destroy them...."

Sin had run its course. The evils wrought by the Canaanites and Amorites caused the Lord to given them over to a hardness of heart (cf. Romans 1:18-19, 24-32). In the end the judgment of God came upon them, and their hearts were so hardened by sin they never thought of repentance (cf. Hebrews 10:32).[9]

Lastly Joshua and the Israelites attacked the cities of the Anakim (11:21-23). The Anakim were warriors of great renown. Their huge size had been the primary cause of the

---

8. Y. Aharoni, *The Land of the Bible: A Historical Geography*. Rev. and enlarged ed. (Philadelphia: Westminster, 1979), 238-39. Other information about these sites can be obtained from M. C. Tenney's *Zondervan Pictorial Encyclopedia of the Bible* (Grand Rapids: Zondervan, 1989), 5 vols.; Rasmussen, *The NIV Atlas of the Bible*, 93-102; and N. Na'aman, *Borders and Districts in Biblical Historiography*, JBS 4 (Jerusalem: Simon, 1986), 119-43.
9. See the excellent article by J. F. Walvoord in *The Theological Workbook*, by D. K. Campbell et al (Nashville: Word, 2000), 150.

Israelite's fearfulness in the wilderness (Numbers 13:22, 28, 32-33). As a result God's people rebelled against Moses and doubted His ability to give them the land. It is with a touch of poetic justice that this account of Joshua's victories should conclude with Israel's defeat of these greatly feared adversaries.

Victories Won by Moses, 12:1-6. There had always been a fear that those tribes that had been given an inheritance in Transjordan would (1) forget their ties to the rest of God's people and in time drift away from their relational and spiritual obligations, or (2) be looked upon by their brethren in Canaan with disfavor. To safeguard against this happening and preserve the unity of God's people the historian wisely included the victories won under Moses' leadership.

This section begins with a summary of the victories over formidable foes living east of the River Jordan. "Now these are the kings of the land whom the sons of Israel defeated, and whose land they possessed beyond the Jordan toward the sunrise, from the valley of the Arnon as far as Mount Hermon, and all the Arabah to the east:

"Sihon king of the Amorites, who lived in Heshbon, and ruled from Aroer, which is on the edge of the valley of the Arnon, both the middle of the valley and half of Gilead, even as far as the brook Jabbok, the border of the sons of Ammon; and the Arabah as far as the Sea of Chinneroth toward the east, and as far as the sea of the Arabah, even the Salt Sea, eastward toward Beth-jeshimoth, and on the south, at the foot of the slopes of Pisgah.

"And the territory of Og king of Bashan, one of the remnant of Rephaim, who lived at Ashtaroth and at Edrei, and ruled over Mount Hermon and Salecah and all Bashan, as far as the border of the Geshurites and the Maacathites, and half of Gilead, as far as the border of Sihon king of Heshbon.

"Moses the servant of Yahweh and the sons of Israel defeated them; and Moses the servant of Yahweh gave it to the Reubenites and the Gadites and the half-tribe of Manasseh as a possession."

The principle kings whom the Israelites defeated were Sihon and Og.

Sihon was an Amorite king whose capital was at Heshbon, near Medeba, not far from Mt. Nebo. He refused to give the Israelites permission to pass through his territory when nearing the Promised Land. When the Israelite host appeared, he gathered his people together and attacked them. The battle was his last. He and all his host were destroyed, and their district from Arnon to Jabbok became the possession of the conqueror, circa 1401 B.C.[10]

Og was the other Amorite whose territory is referred to as Bashan. He ruled over sixty cities, the chief of which were Ashtaroth and Edrei. At the time of the occupation of Canaan, circa 1401 B.C. he was defeated by the Israelites at Edrei and, with his children and people, was exterminated. His many walled cities were taken, and his kingdom was

---

10. *Macmillan Bible Atlas*, 52.

assigned to the Transjordanian tribes, especially the half tribe of Manasseh. Og was a man of giant stature, and Moses spoke of his iron bedstead that was nine cubits (13.5 feet) long by four cubits (6 feet) wide. He was one of the last representatives of the giant race of Rephaim.

Victories Won by Joshua, 12:7-24. The historian next passes on to give us a kaleidoscopic view of the victories won by Joshua. He begins, "Now these are the kings of the land whom Joshua and the sons of Israel defeated beyond the Jordan toward the west, from Baal-gad in the valley of Lebanon even as far as Mount Halak, which rises toward Seir; and Joshua gave it to the tribes of Israel as a possession according to their divisions, in the hill country, in the lowland, in the Arabah, on the slopes, and in the wilderness, and in the Negev; the Hittite, the Amorite and the Canaanite, the Perizzite, the Hivite and the Jebusite." This is followed by an enumeration of the thirty-one kingdoms that were conquered (12:9-24).[11]

In reviewing these chapters we find that they form a necessary introduction to the next section of the book, namely, the division of the land (13:1–21:45). Then, as we push back our chairs and ask ourselves what we have learned from our cursory investigation of this data, we take note of the faithfulness of God. He had promised the land to Abraham and his descendants, and now His people were in possession of it. His power had been evident in giving His people the victory over forces much more powerful than their own. He had not always followed the same strategy,

---

11. Howard, *Joshua*, 286-89.

but showed that He could defeat His enemies by any means. At Jericho His people merely walked around the city; at Ai they set an ambush behind the city; at Gibeon He sent a hailstorm to decimate the enemy, and also caused the sun and moon to remain in their respective orbits; and at Merom He handed over the Canaanite coalition to His people without miraculous intervention. All of these encounters reminded God's people of the power of their God, and demonstrated to the people of the land the powerlessness of their gods.

Though there are many who decry God's harsh treatment of those living in Canaan, the fact remains that they had become so hardened in their sinful ways that punishment was inevitable. And we need to take this to heart, for within our society many of the same sins are acceptable and there are many who believe that they can sin with impunity.

We also find how God graciously confirmed Joshua's leadership (e.g., 6:27). And Joshua obeyed the Lord implicitly (10:14). Few of our leaders today adhere to what the Lord has revealed in His book, the Bible. We should not be surprised, therefore, when those in positions of responsibility appear powerless and ineffective. But we do not have to languish in despondency. The book of Joshua shows us how to be effective leaders in the midst of strong opposition.

But is it possible to discern Joshua's leadership style?[12]

---

12. J. M. Boice, *Joshua* (Old Tappan, NJ: Revell, 1989), 123-27, provides a seminal overview.

It should constantly be borne in mind that leadership which is evil, while it may succeed temporarily, always carries with it the seeds of its own destruction. Both kinds of leadership, the good and the bad, need to have courage and demonstrate the will to exercise leadership. However, in no case will good results be obtained unless the leader is a man who can be looked up to, whose personal judgment is trusted, and who can inspire and warm the hearts of those he leads.

Sound, successful leadership is based on truth and character. A leader must himself be the servant of truth, and he must make that truth the focus of a common purpose. He must also be able to see his problems truly and wholly, and then have the force of character necessary to inspire others to follow him with confidence. And when all is said and done, the true leader must be able to dominate, and finally master, the events that surround him.

Joshua possessed these traits, and the Lord used him in a significant way.

CHAPTER 12

THE DIVISION OF THE LAND

Part One

JOSHUA 13:1–21:45

God's Instructions to Joshua, 13:1-7

The celebrated English novelist Somerset Maugham was being honored on the occasion of his eightieth birthday. After his friends had heaped praise upon him, he rose to give a speech. He began by saying, "There are many virtues to growing old," then he paused and looked down at the table. The pause grew uncomfortably long. Maugham fumbled with his notes, looked around the room, and shifted uneasily from one foot to the other as guests exchanged embarrassed glances. Then clearing his throat Maugham said with a twinkle in his eye, "I'm just trying to remember what they are."

Our chapter opens with God's words to Joshua, "You are old and advanced in years, and very much of the land remains to be possessed."[1] At first glance this sounds like a rebuke. In 11:23 we read, "So Joshua took the whole land,

---

1. Blaikie, *Joshua*, 249-55, has described Joshua's old age in a way that cannot be improved! As always his insights are worthy of serious reflection.

according to all that Yahweh had spoken to Moses, and Joshua gave it for an inheritance to Israel according to their divisions by their tribes. Thus, the land had rest from war." How are we to reconcile these two statements?

Joshua had been emimently successful, but now he was old. He would live on for another ten or twelve years, but the time had come for a change in leadership. The leaders of the different tribes were now to step forward and assume responsibility for the success of their people.

Because of this transition in leadership, we do well to remind ourselves of the divisions of this book. We began with the Invasion of the Land, 1:1–5:15. This was followed by the chapters dealing with the Conquest of the Land, 6:1–12:45. Now that the land has been subdued, Joshua was being asked to Distribute the Land, 13:1–22:34.

But what are we to make of God's statement that "very much land remains to be possessed"? Though the Lord was very specific, the land that remained to be possessed was limited to "all the regions of the Philistines and all those of the Geshurites; from the Shihor which is east of Egypt, even as far as the border of Ekron to the north (it is counted as Canaanite); the five lords of the Philistines: the Gazite, the Ashdodite, the Ashkelonite, the Gittite, the Ekronite, the Avvite to the south, all the land of the Canaanite." The land still to be possessed included a section of land the northern edge of which extended to Lebo-Hamath, almost 50 miles north of Damascus, to "Mearah that belongs to the Sidonians, as far as Aphek, to the border of the Amorite; and the land of the Gebalite, and all of Lebanon, toward the east, from Baal-gad below Mount Hermon as far as Lebo-hamath." Then God continued, "All the inhabitants of the hill country from Lebanon as far as Misrephoth-maim, all the Sidonians, *I will drive them out from before the sons of Israel; only allot it to Israel for an inheritance as I have commanded you.*[2] Now therefore, apportion this land for an inheritance to the nine tribes and the half-tribe of Manasseh" (emphasis added).[3]

Inheritance in Transjordan, 13:8-33

The data given here has been presented before. Now, however, the dimensions of each tribe's territory are made specific. It is with regret that we note verse 13: "But the sons of Israel did not dispossess the Geshurites [northeast of the Sea of Galilee] or the Maacathites [north of Geshur]; for Geshur and Maacath live among Israel until this day." Apparently some inertia came over the people, and they may have considered that they already had enough land for their needs so why continue to exert themselves.

There are constant references in the text to the victories God had given Israel through Moses, and these must have been of encouragement to God's people. Some indication of the significance of the defeat of Sihon and Og[4] is to be

---

2. The "I" is emphatic. God would give them the power to drive out the people.
3. The easiest way to ascertain the extent of the land to be possessed is to consult Rasmussen's *NIV Atlas of the Bible*, 101-02; the *Macmillan Bible Atlas*, 50-51; and Y. Aharoni, *The Land of the Bible*, 233-39.

gleaned from references to them in the book of Psalms (cf. Psalms 135:10-12; 136:17-22).

Twice we are told that the Levites did not receive an inheritance because the Lord was their inheritance (13:14, 33; cf. Deuteronomy 18:1). Levi's inheritance consisted of the offerings by fire (i.e., a portion of the sacrifices offered at the central sanctuary), and later we will read that they were given 48 cities with the surrounding land so that they could have their flocks and herds graze on the land. The purpose of dispersing the Levites among the people was to have them teach the people God's Word.

There is also in the text a parenthetical reminder about Balaam (13:22). From Numbers 31:8, the death of Balaam took place in the days of Moses on the border of the tribes of Reuben and Gad. Mention is made of him now to serve as a warning to Israel. While Balaam's public discourses spoke eloquently of Israel in the plan and purpose of God, and of their glorious privileges, yet for the sake of monetary gain he explained how the Lord's favor could be withdrawn from His people. His recommendation was simple. He encouraged Balak, king of Moab, to have beautiful Moabite girls tempt Israelite men to engage in idolatrous feasts and sensual practices. These acts, Balaam counseled, would cause the Lord to punish His people. Balaam probably gained his

---

4. Cf. J. R. Bartlett, *Vetus Testamentum* 20 (1970), 257-77; A. Bergman, *Journal of the American Oriental Society* 54 (1934), 169-77; J. Simons, *Palestine Exploration Quarterly* 79 (1947), 27-39.

reward, but he did not live to enjoy it. He died soon after in a battle against Israel.

The reminder of the fate of this prophet from the Euphrates causes us to recall the fact that there are people even in our day whose gifts are beyond question, yet who are more interested in personal gain than in serving the Lord. They are found in all branches of the Christian church (Jude 1:12-13), and we need to be on our guard against them.

The Inheritance in Canaan, 14:1–19:51

Introduction, 14:1-5. With the tribes of Reuben, Gad, and the half tribe of Manasseh settled in Transjordan, Joshua, aided by Eleazar the priest and the leaders of the nine and a half tribes, began to focus their attention on the territory west of the Jordan River. Inheritance was to be determined by the casting of lots.

The Inheritance of Judah, 14:6–15:63. As mention of Balaam served as a warning to the eastern tribes, so mention of Caleb serves as an encouragement to those who settled in the west. But who was Caleb? And what did he do that caused his life and actions to be preserved forever on the pages of God's Word?

Caleb had been born in slavery. He grew to manhood knowing what it was like to toil all day in the heat of the Egyptian sun, to have perspiration run in rivulets down his body, to force his aching muscles to carry clay and mix mortar, and to feel the sting of the taskmaster's whip on his back. He knew the weariness of endless servile work, and this made the promise of an inheritance in Canaan precious to him.

Caleb was not an Israelite by birth. He is introduced to us as the "son of Jephunneh, the Kennizite," and the implication is that he was a descendant of Kenaz, the son of Esau. It is probable that Jephunneh became a believer in the God of Israel and married into the tribe of Judah. He taught his son, Caleb, to believe in the promise that God had made to Abraham, and as a young lad Caleb looked forward to the time when the Israelites would be restored to the land that had been promised to them.

As Caleb attained manhood, he became an outstanding leader. The families of the tribe of Judah recognized the qualities of honesty and courage, self-discipline and decisiveness which were inherent in him, and they made him the *rosh,* "prince," of their tribe.

Later a man named Moses demanded of Pharaoh that he let God's people go. Pharaoh refused, and a series of plagues made the lives of the Egyptians miserable.[5] Then on a never-to-be-forgotten night Pharaoh ordered their departure, and the Red Sea opened before them. A few weeks later God constituted His people a nation at Mt.

---

5. Readers will find J. J. Davis' *Moses and the Gods of Egypt* (Grand Rapids: Baker, 1977), 331pp., an excellent resource; and those fortunate enough to have T. S. Millington's *Signs and Wonders in the Land of Ham: A Description of the Ten Plagues of Egypt* (London: Murray, 1873), 239pp., will find that the author has included many apt descriptions of the events that transpired when Moses confronted Pharaoh on God's behalf.

Sinai, and after building the Tabernacle the sons of Israel set off for the Promised Land.

Stopping at the southern border of Canaan, Moses sent spies into the country to ascertain the strengths and weaknesses of the people, and bring back evidence of the land's productivity (Numbers 13:1–14:45). Caleb was chosen as one of the spies. After six weeks of traveling up and down the country, they returned. The report given to Moses was that the land contained everything they had been promised, but ten of the spies filled the hearts of the people with fear. They described the giant Anakim whom they had seen and exaggerated the strength of the cities by claiming that their walls reached up to heaven.

Caleb and Joshua stood firm against this false report, but the ten spies turned the hearts of the people against Moses. These cowardly spies died that day in a plague before the Lord, and the people who did not believe that the Lord could give them the land spent the next 38 years wandering aimlessly in the desert. Worst of all, Caleb and Joshua were kept out of their inheritance because of the unbelief of the others.

As we take a closer look at 14:6-15 we find that Caleb was a man who wholly followed the Lord his God. The biblical historian, writing under inspiration of the Holy Spirit, records what happened. "Then the sons of Judah drew near to Joshua in Gilgal, and Caleb the son of Jephunneh the Kennizite said to him, 'You know the word which Yahweh spoke to Moses the man of God concerning you and me in Kadesh-Barnea. I was forty years old when Moses the servant of Yahweh sent me from Kadesh-Barnea to spy out the land, and I brought word back to him as it was in my heart. Nevertheless my brethren who went up with me made the heart of the people melt with fear; *but I followed Yahweh my God fully.* So Moses swore on that day, saying, "Surely the land on which your foot has trodden will be an inheritance to you and to your children forever, because *you have followed Yahweh my God fully.*" Now behold, Yahweh has let me live, just as He spoke, these forty-five years, from the time that Yahweh spoke this word to Moses, when Israel walked in the wilderness; and now behold, I am eighty-five years old today. I am still as strong today as I was in the day Moses sent me; as my strength was then, so my strength is now, for war and for going out and coming in. Now then, give me this hill country about which Yahweh spoke on that day, for you heard on that day that Anakim were there, with great fortified cities; perhaps Yahweh will be with me, and I will drive them out as Yahweh has spoken.' So Joshua blessed him and gave Hebron to Caleb the son of Jephunneh for an inheritance. Therefore, Hebron became the inheritance of Caleb the son of Jephunneh the Kennizite until this day, because *he followed Yahweh God of Israel fully.* Now the name of Hebron was formerly Kiriath-arba; for Arba was the greatest man among the Anakim. Then the land had rest from war."

Caleb's thankfulness to God for past mercies and humility in going to attack Hebron are noteworthy, and from his experience we learn several important lessons. First, in retrospect, the unbelief of the ten spies robbed that generation of the blessings God stood ready to give them. In this we are reminded of an incident in the life of the Lord Jesus.

He could do no mighty work in Nazareth because of the unbelief of the people (Mark 6:5). The experience of Caleb may also answer (at least in part) the question of why we see little of God's activity in our churches. The unbelief of the spies did not negate God's promise to His people, but it did deprive an entire generation of their enjoyment of their inheritance. Unbelief limits God's power and robs us of His blessing.

Caleb exercised patience during the 38 years in the desert. He did not give way to complaining. He could have bemoaned the fact that his most productive years were being wasted, or blamed others for the predicament in which he found himself. Instead, he placed his confidence in God's promise and persevered without losing sight of the goal–his possession of an inheritance in the Land of Promise.

Finally, when the last of the faithless Israelites had died, Joshua led the Israelites across the River Jordan: the conquest of the land had begun. And when the land had been conquered, Caleb with the leaders of the tribe of Judah came to Joshua and asked that he be given the inheritance that Moses had promised him.[6]

---

6. Three separate passages deal with the conquest of Hebron (Joshua 14:6-15; 15:13; and Judges 1:10). From these Scriptures the victory over the Anakim is ascribed to Caleb, the tribe of Judah, and the Israelites. Confusion only exists in the minds of those who find fault with the Bible and look for supposed discrepancies. In reality no contradictions exist. Everything depends on the perspective of the writer.

In this we find another important biblical principle: God's promises are sure, but they must be claimed by faith. So Caleb came to Joshua and said, "Now then, give me this mountain" (14:12, AV). And having been given Hebron as his inheritance, and with true dependence upon the Lord, Caleb went up to this citadel and captured it. Arba may have died in the years since Kadesh-Barnea, but his sons were still living there. We do not know how Caleb conquered the city, but he won a decisive victory and it became his inheritance

In the final analysis Caleb proves that God is faithful to His promises in spite of the delays that often leave us frustrated and resentful.

CHAPTER 13

THE DIVISION OF THE LAND

Part Two

JOSHUA 13:1–21:45

The Inheritance in Canaan, 14:1–19:51, cont.

With these chapters we come to the distribution of the land. The tribes of Reuben, Gad, and half the tribe of Manasseh have already received their inheritance in Gilead. Now the territory from Dan to Beersheba and from the River Jordan to the Great Sea (i.e., the Mediterranean) is to be divided between the remaining nine and a half tribes. Each of the tribes is to come before the Lord at Shiloh and there Joshua, Eleazar, and the heads of the tribes will supervise the casting of lots to determine each tribe's inheritance.

Though the narrative appears boring, there are important principles in it that repay careful consideration. First, there is value to having distinct tribal lands.[1] This allows for diversity within an overall unity. Each tribe could main-

---

1. T. Smith, *Joshua*, 213-46, builds upon Genesis 49:1-27, and by combining Jacob's intuitive understanding of each of his sons (including his "adopted" sons, Ephraim and Manasseh) with their later history, he provides a discerning analysis of each of the twelve tribes.

tain its individual character, while at the same time being available for a joint venture should a need arise. Second, it has been estimated that each household would receive about forty-two acres of farmland. The ancient Romans believed that a citizen and his family could survive with seven acres. It will readily be seen that in God's economy He intended for each family to have enough and to spare.

The Inheritance of Judah, 14:6–15:63, cont. After Caleb had been given his inheritance, the tribe of Judah was given its land (15:1-63; see also Judges 1:8-18). The easiest way to ascertain the extent of the territory assigned to them is to consult Carl G. Rasmussen's atlas and the section entitled the "Settlement in the Land of Canaan."[2]

After conquering Hebron, Caleb proceeded on to Kiriath-sepher (the "city of books"–what we would refer to today as a "university town" that was probably a center devoted to the study of occultism). And he said, "The one who attacks Kiriath-sepher and captures it, I will give him Achsah my daughter as a wife. And Othniel the son of Kenaz, the [half-] brother of Caleb, captured it; so he gave him Achsah his daughter as a wife." Now after their marriage, when she came to live with him, she persuaded him to ask her father for a field. (Othniel apparently did so, and Caleb gave him and Achsah the land of the Negev.) Achsah, however, was farsighted. She realized that water was essential to survival in the long dry summer months and so, when she saw her father "she alighted from the donkey[3] [to

---

2. Rasmussen, *NIV Atlas of the Bible*, 96-97.

petition her father for some additional land], and Caleb said to her, 'What do you want?' Then she said, 'Give me a blessing; since you have given me the land of the Negev, give me also springs of water.' So he gave her the upper springs and the lower springs" (15:16-19).

From this incident the Irish theologian, Dr. Andrew R. Fausset, draws a picture of prayer. Achsah's request was based upon her relationship with her father. She knew him to be large-hearted and gracious. When she came to him she *tzanach,* eagerly "leapt" from her donkey (which in itself was a token of reverence), and when her father asked what she wanted, her request was clear and direct. "You have given me the [dry] southland, give me also springs of water." And Caleb gave her the upper and lower springs.[4] Everything that Caleb did was similar to what our heavenly Father has done and still does for us!

Judah's territory was large and included many important cities. The people of this tribe successfully possessed the land assigned to them, except for the city of Jebus. "Now as for the Jebusites, the inhabitants of Jerusalem, the sons of Judah could not drive them out; so the Jebusites live with the sons of Judah at Jerusalem until this day" (15:63).

The Inheritance of Ephraim and Manasseh, 16:1–17:18. The next distribution of land was made to the tribes

---

3. Achsah was courteous. Her attitude was typical of one petitioning a superior.
4. A. R. Fausset, *Expository Commentary on the Book of Judges* (Minneapolis: James & Klock, 1976), 21.

of Ephraim and Manasseh. Ephraim and Manasseh were the sons of Joseph. Jacob adopted them as his sons (Genesis 48:5), and in time they became two large tribes. Because Levi did not receive an inheritance among the tribes, the inclusion of Ephraim and Manasseh preserved the twelve-tribe division. Ephraim was allotted the southern part of the hill country, from the River Jordan to the Mediterranean.[5]

At first sight the territory assigned this tribe appears more than adequate, but we find that the men of Ephraim did not exert themselves as the men of Judah had done. They did not drive out the Canaanites that lived in Gezer (16:10), but complained that the Canaanites had chariots of iron.

But what of Caleb's example? He was a man of faith. He had gone up against the giants who lived in Hebron, and the Lord had given them into his hand. Surely God could do the same for the sons of Joseph? But there was something else. The men of Ephraim prefaced their petition for more land (17:15-18) by bewailing the fact that they had only been given one lot and one portion (17:14). This was plainly a reference to Manasseh who had also received an inheritance east of the River Jordan. Though this request came from Joshua's own tribe, he did not grant it. Instead, he told his kinsmen to go into the hill country and clear away the forest. In other words, if they wanted more land they must work for it.

---

5. See Rasmussen, *NIV Atlas to the Bible*, 96-97; see also Aharoni, *The Land of the Bible*, 257.

As the apostle Paul later taught, "godliness with contentment is great gain" (1 Timothy 6:6).

The half tribe of Manasseh was allotted land that enabled them to control the northern part of central Canaan.

Of particular interest is the request of the five daughters of Zelophehad.[6] Zelophehad had no sons. His daughters had approached Moses in the desert with the request that he rule on whether they could inherit land when their father died (cf. Numbers 26:33; 27:1-11; 36:11; Joshua 17:3). Moses had laid this matter before the Lord, and He had ruled that they could inherit within their tribe. The only limitation placed upon them was that they were also to marry within their tribe, which they did.

We cannot conclude our perusal of these chapters without taking note of the failure of these tribes to trust the Lord for victory. God's promise of help was as explicit as His command for these nations to be destroyed (cf. Exodus 23:23-33; 34:11-16; Deuteronomy 7:1-6). Apparently inertia led first to an uneasy coexistence, and then to full acceptance with intermarriage taking place. It wasn't long before God's people began worshiping the gods of the Canaanites.

Division of the Land Among the Remaining Tribes (18:1–19:51). Once the "Tent of Meeting" (i.e., the Tabernacle) had been set up at Shiloh, we would have expected

---

6. J. Pedersen, *Israel, Its Life and Culture,* 4 vols in 2 (Oxford: University Press, 1926), 1-2:94-96; N. H. Snaith, *Vetus Testamentum* 16 (1966), 124-27; J. Weingreen, *Vetus Testamentum* 16 (1966), 518-22.

the other tribes to rush headlong into the vacant land and seize an inheritance for themselves. Instead we find that they were content to be squatters. Joshua had to indict them for being slackers (18:3). As a result of their lethargy they were impugning the character of the One who had promised to give them the land.

This sorry state of affairs could not be allowed to continue. Joshua, therefore, summoned the whole congregation of the sons of Israel to assemble at Shiloh. There he challenged them with the fact that their dalliance was out of character with what the Lord required of them. Then he commanded them to provide three men from each of the remaining seven tribes to walk through the land and write a description of it according to their inheritance. This done, they were to return to him and he would divide the unassigned territory among them (18:1-5).

Even in his old age Joshua was a man of action. The tribes selected their representatives, and they left to map out the remaining parcels of land. When these early cartographers[7] returned to Joshua, they gave him the book they had written. The remaining tribes were then assigned a portion of the land by means of lots (18:6, 8, 10). Such a proceeding prevented future complaining and/or discontent among God's people.

Benjamin received its inheritance in the hill country sandwiched between Judah and Ephraim (18:11-28). Simeon's land was within the tribe of Judah (19:1-9), and included some significant towns and cities. Zebulun's portion was in southern Galilee (19:10-16). Issachar was given land at the eastern end of the Valley of Jezreel.[8] Asher's grant stretched from Mount Carmel in the south to Sidon in the north. Naphtali's heritage (19:32-39) lay between Mount Tabor in the south and the River Litani in the north. And Dan's original inheritance was squeezed between the tribes of Benjamin, Ephraim and Judah (19:40-48).

With the allocation complete, Joshua encouraged each tribe to go and possess its land.

Lastly, we are told of the inheritance of Joshua (19:49-50) with 19:51 serving as a summary. There is something very instructive in the way this section begins and ends. It began with Caleb receiving Hebron as his inheritance, and it closes with Joshua receiving Timnath-serah as his inheritance. Both men had gone from Kadesh-Barnea with the original spies to gain information about the land of Canaan. Caleb and Joshua had brought back a positive report. The other ten spies had brought the majority report, but they did

---

7. For information about the portions of land assigned the seven tribes, see Aharoni, *The Land of the Bible* (1979), 248-62, and the maps in Rasmussen's *NIV Atlas of the Bible*, 98-101. It should come as no surprise that negative Bible critics have debated the accuracy of the biblical record, some even claiming that the record was only compiled many years (in fact, centuries) after the time of Joshua. This is in spite of the repeated statement that something continues to exist "to this day" or "until this day." See C. F. Burney, *Israel's Settlement in Canaan, the Biblical Tradition and its Historical Background* (London: Oxford U. P., 1918), 104pp. + 6 maps; and M. Weippert, *The Settlement of the Israelite Tribes in Palestine*. Studies in Biblical Theology, 21, trans. by J. D. Martin (Naperville: Allenson, 1971), 171pp.
8. Also known as the Valley of the Esdraelon.

not believe that the Lord could give them the land. They had died in a plague that day, and the unbelieving Israelites over the age of 20, who favored going back to Egypt, perished in the wilderness during the 38 years of fruitless wandering from place to place (Numbers 13–14).

In this chapter we find that God is faithful. Both Caleb and Joshua are rewarded exactly as God had promised years earlier (cf. Numbers 14:24, 30)! His word is sure. There are times when it is difficult to exercise faith in His promises, but when this happens we should remember the example of Caleb and Joshua.

The Cities of Refuge, 20:1-9

Some years ago my wife and I visited the "Big Island" of Hawaii. We found that whatever sightseeing we did had to be done before 11:00 A.M. for torrential rains then swept over the island every morning about that time. One place close to our hotel was *Pu'uhonua*, the City of Refuge.

In ancient times Hawaiians lived under strict laws. Commoners could not get too close to their chief, nor were they allowed to touch any of his possessions, walk in his footsteps or even let their shadow touch the royal grounds. The penalty for violating a sacred *kapu* (taboo) was death.

Breaking a *kapu* was believed to incur the wrath of the gods. Hawaiians often chased down an offender and swiftly put him to death unless he could reach a *pu'uhonua* or place of refuge. There he could be absolved by a *kahuna* (priest) in a purification ceremony before returning home with his transgression forgiven.

Joshua appointed six cities of refuge in keeping with the instruction God had given Moses (Numbers 35:11-12; Deuteronomy 4:41-43; 19:1-14), three cities on each side of the River Jordan. These cities were easily accessible so that a person who had accidently committed manslaughter could flee there. All these cities were Levitical cities (see chapter 21). The person who had inadvertently killed someone could then recount his case before elders of the city, and if they found that he was not guilty of premeditated murder they would allow him to take up residence in their city. The man would later have to stand trial in a city near where the incident occurred (cf. Numbers 35:25-34). If found innocent he would then have to return to the city of refuge where he was compelled to stay until the death of the high priest. Only then could he return to his home.

The Cities of the Levites, 21:1-45

We have repeatedly read that the Levites were not given an inheritance like the other tribes, for the Lord was their inheritance. However, Joshua and Eleazar did assign the three divisions of the tribe of Levi–the Kohathites, the Gershonites, and the Merarites--48 towns or cities with their pasture lands.[9] This does not mean that the Israelites to whom these cities had been assigned were dispossessed of their inheritance, but only that some of Israel's religious leaders came and lived among them. This system insured

---

9. See Rasmussen, *NIV Atlas of the Bible*, 102-03.

that there was a continuous spiritual influence over all the people.[10]

In the plan and purpose of God the tribe of Levi was not only to serve in the central sanctuary but also to be teachers of the Law (Deuteronomy 33:8-11; see also 2 Chronicles 17:7-9; 35:3; Nehemiah 8:7-9).[11]

This section closes with a summary: *"So Yahweh gave Israel all the land which He had sworn to give to their fathers, and they possessed it and lived in it. And Yahweh gave them rest on every side, according to all that He had sworn to their fathers, and no one of all their enemies stood before them; Yahweh gave all their enemies into their hand. Not one of the good promises which Yahweh had made to the house of Israel failed; all came to pass"* (21:43-45).

In this statement the biblical historian steps back and surveys God's promise from the time of Abraham to the settlement of the tribes. He sees how God had dispossessed nations greater and mightier than Israel in order to give to His people the land that He had sworn to Abraham. He had been faithful in all He had done. None of His promises had failed. His gifts to His chosen people were threefold: (1) a

---

10. Charles Ryrie in the *Ryrie Study Bible, Expanded Edition*, 363, has estimated that no Israelite lived more than ten miles from a city in which Levites lived.
11. Unhappily, the priesthood deteriorated until a time came when God, speaking through His prophet, Malachi, had to rebuke their faithlessness (see Malachi 2:4-7)!

possession, (2) rest, and (3) peace. All that remained was for Israel to respond to Him in gratitude and devotion.

CHAPTER 14

JOSHUA'S FAREWELL MESSAGES

Part One

JOSHUA 22:1-34

Joshua's Farewell to the Transjordanian Tribes, 22:1-8

With this chapter the reader senses that the writer is bringing the history of the conquest of Canaan to a close. He had previously written, "So Yahweh gave Israel all the land which He had sworn to give to their fathers, and they possessed it and lived in it. And He gave them rest on every side, according to all that He had sworn to their fathers, and no one of all their enemies stood before them; Yahweh gave all their enemies into their hand. *Not one of the good promises which Yahweh had made to the house of Israel failed; all came to pass*" (Joshua 21:43-45, emphasis added).[1]

---

1. So far the book of Joshua has been concerned with God's initiatives. For example, He enabled the Israelites to cross the Jordan; He enabled them to take Jericho; He gave them victories over the people of the land; He supervised the division of the land; and He provided cities of refuge. Now, in these remaining chapters, Joshua undertakes to admonish the Israelites to obey and serve the Lord.

Joshua's Commendation, 22:1-4. Joshua began by summoning to him the tribes of Reuben, Gad and the half-tribe of Manasseh, and he thanked them for the seven years of service they had given their brethren. He began with praise for their obedience: "You have kept all that Moses the servant of Yahweh commanded you, and have listened to my voice in all that I commanded you." Next he commended their loyalty: "You have not forsaken your brethren these many days to this day, but have kept the charge of the commandment of Yahweh your God. And now Yahweh your God has given rest to your brethren, as He spoke to them; therefore turn now and go to your tents, to the land of your possession, which Moses the servant of Yahweh gave you beyond the Jordan" (22:2-4).

The obedience of the two and a half tribes was threefold: to God, to Moses, and to Joshua. Now these warriors are complimented by their general and honorably discharged. With light hearts and loaded with spoil they re-cross the River Jordan en route to their homes.

Joshua's Encouragement, 22:5a. In sending these soldiers back to their wives and children, Joshua admonished them to continue to follow the Lord, and to share the spoils of war with those who had protected their loved ones during the years of fighting. His final charge was clear: "Only be very careful to observe the commandment and the law which Moses the servant of Yahweh commanded you, to love Yahweh your God and walk in all His ways and keep His commandments and hold fast to Him and serve Him with all your heart and with all your soul.... Return to your tents with great riches and with very much livestock, with silver, gold, bronze, iron, and with very many clothes; divide the spoil of your enemies with your brethren" (Joshua 22:5, 8).

Selfishness might very easily cause them to keep all the spoils of war for themselves. After all, they had endured forced marches at night and faced the dangers of hand-to-hand combat. Why shouldn't they keep all the spoils for themselves? But their brethren had stayed at home, protected their families, and toiled in plowing the fields and keeping the sheep and goats and cows safe from wild beasts. They deserved some "remuneration" for their diligent efforts. Generosity and tangible expressions of thankfulness are seldom out of place.

Joshua's Exhortation, 22:5b. Joshua also counseled those who were now taking up residence in Transjordan to remain loyal to the Lord. During times of prosperity there is always the danger that the hearts of people will grow cold, and that they will drift away from true devotion to what they know to be right. Joshua also knew that the nation had not been completely weaned away from idolatry (cf. 24:14, see also Amos 5:26), and so he warned them against being seduced into following the gods of the heathen, for this would incur God's judgment. And so he exhorted them to be very careful to observe the commandment of the Lord and His law which Moses the servant of Yahweh had given them, namely, to love Yahweh their God and walk in all His ways and keep His commandments. Joshua also encouraged them to hold fast to the Lord and serve Him with all their heart and with all their soul.

How simple this all sounds, and yet how difficult to perform. Faithfulness to the Lord necessitates continued diligence. It requires of us the same commitment to God's Word that the Lord required of Joshua (1:8). And it is the only way to continuously walk in His ways, keep His commandments, hold fast to Him, and serve Him with all of our being!

Joshua's Blessing, 22:6-8. Then Joshua blessed them. In Scripture we are told that "the lesser is blessed by the greater" (Hebrews 7:7). Blessing is the enrichment of someone or something beyond what is expected. When applied to people it involves making them happy. For example, in Psalm 1:1, because there is no verb in the original, the truest translation of "How blessed is the man who ..." is "O the *happiness* of the man who ...." Someone who is in vital touch with the Members of the Godhead has the God-given power to bless others. Others may mouth the words, but they lack the unction of the Holy Spirit. Joshua was God's representative to the people, and he possessed the intrinsic power to bless others.[2]

Misunderstanding and Crisis, 22:9-24.

It's Development, 22:9-12. We cannot tell how long a time elapsed between Joshua's meeting with the two and a half tribes and the misunderstanding that arose over the altar they built on the banks of the River Jordan. Inasmuch as

---

2. Cf. Butler, *Joshua,* 245.

Joshua is not mentioned in these verses we presume that he had retired to his home in Timnath-serah.

"The children of Reuben, the children of Gad, and half the tribe of Manasseh returned [to their homes], and departed from the children of Israel at Shiloh, which is in the land of Canaan, to go to the country of Gilead, to the land of their possession, which they had obtained according to the word of Yahweh by the hand of Moses. And when they came to the region of the Jordan which is in the land of Canaan, the children of Reuben, the children of Gad, and half the tribe of Manasseh built a great, impressive altar[3] there by the Jordan" (22:9-10, 28b). It was in all probability erected on the western plain of the River Jordan.

Someone brought word to Shiloh that their brethren had built this altar, and either the person bringing the news or someone else added a deleterious value judgment that implied the eastern tribes had already apostatized from the Lord. We know that the eastern tribes were motivated by a desire to preserve their unity with the nine and a half tribes in the west. The rumor, however, was readily accepted by the rest of the people and the whole congregation gathered together in a war council (22:12).[4]

We are not told that the people asked counsel of the Lord. Fortunately Eleazar the priest was there, and he proposed that a delegation representing the western tribes be

---

3. Various translations have been offered, but the one that best fits the context is "altar."
4. G. Bush, *Joshua*, 193-94.

sent to inquire into the purpose of the altar. Phineas, Eleazar's son, was with them.

The Accusation, 22:13-20. The opening salvo on the part of the western tribes was fierce and assumed that their Transjordanian brethren were guilty of the vilest deeds ever to disgrace their nation (22:15-18). They went so far as to charge their brethren with divisiveness and rebellion against the Lord. The events at Baal-peor (Numbers 25:1-9),[5] when the Israelites had apostatized from the Lord and sacrificed to Baal, were still fresh in the minds of the people, and so was God's fierce judgment! The delegation from Shiloh did not want a repetition of this kind of event, for it would involve all of God's people in the resulting punishment.

The hostile accusation on the part of the representatives of the western tribes could have resulted in civil war. However, someone (possibly Phineas) who was not as hotheaded as his companions was more conciliatory. He said, "If, however, the land of your possession is unclean, then cross into the land of the possession of Yahweh, where Yahweh's Tabernacle stands, and take possession among us. Only do not rebel against Yahweh, or rebel against us by building an altar for yourselves, besides the altar of Yahweh our God" (22:19). God's people had learned from their mistakes, and this spokesman then added the illustration of Achan (7:1-

---

5. The transgression of the Israelites at Baal-peor and their subsequent punishment made such a lasting impression on the nation that it was even mentioned by the prophet Hosea approximately 675 years later (see Hosea 9:10),

26). He had disobeyed the command of the Lord, and the whole nation had been rendered powerless as a result.

The Defense, 22:21-24. After this severe charge, it may have taken a few seconds for those living in Gilead to recover from their surprise. Their opening statement reveals how deeply the misunderstanding of their brethren had hurt them. "The Mighty One, God, [even] Yahweh, the Mighty One, God, [even] Yahweh! He knows, and may Israel itself know. If it was in rebellion, or if in an unfaithful act against Yahweh do not save us this day! If we have built us an altar to turn away from following Yahweh, or if to offer a burnt offering or grain offering on it, or if to offer sacrifices of peace offerings on it, may Yahweh Himself require it. But truly we have done this out of concern, for a reason, saying, 'In time to come your sons may say to our sons, "What have you to do with Yahweh, the God of Israel? For Yahweh has made the Jordan a border between us and you[6], you sons of Reuben and sons of Gad; you have no portion in Yahweh," so your sons may make our sons stop fearing Yahweh.' Therefore we said, 'Let us build an altar, not for burnt offering or for sacrifice; rather it shall be a witness between us and you and between our generations after us, that we are to perform the service of Yahweh before Him with our burnt offerings, and with our sacrifices and with our peace offerings, so that your sons will not say to our sons in time to come, "You have no portion in Yahweh" ... [the altar] it is a witness between us and you'" (22:22-28).

---

6. Cf. T. Smith, *Joshua*, 270-72; cf. D. Jobling, *Journal for the Study of the Old Testament* Supplement 39 (1986), 88-134.

The motivation behind building the altar was one of fear. The eastern tribes were concerned lest in time they cease to be regarded as a part of the nation. The altar was designed as a memorial, nothing more (22:29).

Crisis Resolved, 22:30-34.

Happily, Phineas was among the delegation made up of the heads of every tribe and the leaders of the thousands in Israel. He praised God for their answer. It was clear to him that the motive of the eastern tribes was the preservation of unity so that they and their descendants would always be welcomed at the place where God chose to have His people worship Him. He said, "This day we perceive that Yahweh is among us, because you have not committed this treachery against Him. Now you have delivered the children of Israel out of the hand of Yahweh." Had the motive of the eastern tribes been less pure the result would have resulted in war.

What is important for us to realize is that certain actions taken unilaterally, even those free from ulterior motives, may result in misunderstanding and schism. And if there is no one like Phineas to heal the breach that is forming, then an irreparable rift may be the result.

When Phineas and the leaders of the people returned to Shiloh, they gave a full report to those present. "The word pleased the sons of Israel, and the sons of Israel blessed God; and they did not speak of going up against them in war to destroy the land in which the sons of Reuben and the sons of Gad were living."

The Transjordanian tribes of Reuben and Gad chose to call the altar that they had built *ed*, meaning "witness," saying, "It shall be a witness between us that Yahweh is God." It was to serve as a testimony to the people of Israel on both sides of the River Jordan that the Lord is the one true God and there is no other. It was also designed to declare their intention to pass on to their posterity their belief in the truth about the Lord God in the hope that their children and their children's children would not succumb to idolatry.

From this chapter we glean several important truths, foremost of which is the danger of basing our actions on hearsay.

In classical literature[7] we come across a race of women warriors called Amazons who lived near the Black Sea. They were more than a figment of storytellers' imagination, for history records their invasion of Lycia, attack on Phyrigia, and defeat by Theseus, king of Attica, in the Battle of Thermodon. Of the many stories told about these women one explained the absence of men in their society. According to this tradition, when their husbands were away fighting in a war, a messenger came bringing news of their victory. Among the spoils of war were beautiful women, and each of the soldiers supposedly took one or more of them in marriage.[8] This was only a rumor, but it was

---

7. Primarily in the writings of Homer (Iliad), Herodotus, Diodorus of Sicily, and Plutarch.
8. It was common for soldiers to take women captured in battle as slaves (or perhaps concubines), but not as wives.

believed by their wives. When their husbands came home, their wives arranged for them to be murdered.

A similar story became the basis for Shakespeare's tragedy *Othello*. The Bard showed how dangerous misinformation can be. As a result of cunningly contrived slander Othello murdered his wife Desdemona for her supposed infidelity. Too late he realized what he had done. When he was told that he must be tried for murder, he killed himself.

Slander involves bearing false witness against your neighbor out of malignity or vanity so as to prejudice his fame, safety or welfare. As such it is condemned in Scripture (cf. Exodus 20:16). The principal kinds of slander are: (1) charging others with acts they are not guilty of having committed; (2) affixing odious motives to the actions of individuals; (3) maligning a person's actions by implying that they proceed from evil principles; (4) perverting a man's words or actions disadvantageously; (5) a partial or lame representation of men's discourse or practice, suppressing some part of the truth or concealing some circumstances which ought to be explained; (6) resorting to cunningly contrived suggestions which create prejudice in the minds of hearers; (7) magnifying and aggravating the faults of others; and (8) imputing to a person's practice, judgment, or profession evil consequences which have no foundation in truth.

Those who engage in such acts are guilty of character assassination and inflict untold hurt on the guiltless. In *Othello* people who were innocent died along with the guilty. It is no wonder that Scripture exhorts us to banish from our lives all bitterness and wrath and anger and clamor and *slander*, along with all malice, and to be kind to one another, tender-hearted, forgiving each other, just as God in Christ also has forgiven us (cf. Ephesians 4:31-32; see also Mark 7:20-22; Colossians 3:8; 1 Peter 2:1).

CHAPTER 15

JOSHUA'S FAREWELL MESSAGES

Part Two

JOSHUA 23:1-16

It is customary to treat with respect the last words of a loved one. The person who is dying is soon to be ushered into eternity, and their admonitions in light of special circumstances are designed to encourage us to persevere through life's many vicissitudes.

D. L. Moody was used of God to awaken people in the United States as well as in the United Kingdom to their need of Christ. Over his grave was inscribed the Scriptural promise: "He who does the will of God abides forever."

Dr. Edward Payson, the well-known Congregational preacher, who came to faith in Christ after graduating from Harvard, and whose ministry saw thousands put their trust in Christ for their eternal salvation, encouraged those who remained behind with the words, "I am dying, but God will surely be with you." And on his coffin was inscribed: "Remember the words which I spoke to you while I was present with you."

Leigh Richmond has been forgotten by succeeding generations of Christians. When he came to the end of his earthly pilgrimage he exclaimed, "It will be all confusion."

His wife asked him what would be confusion, and he responded, "The church! There will be confusion in the church." His insight into what would happen in subsequent decades proved true.

When the apostle Paul bade farewell to the Ephesian believers, his last words were, "And now, behold, I know that all of you, among whom I went about preaching the kingdom, will no longer see my face. Therefore, I testify to you this day that ... I did not shrink from declaring to you the whole counsel of God. Be on guard for yourselves and for all the flock, among which the Holy Spirit has made you overseers, to shepherd the church of God which He purchased with His own blood. I know that after my departure savage wolves will come in among you, not sparing the flock, and from among your own selves men will arise, speaking perverse things, to draw away the disciples after them. Therefore be on the alert ..." (Acts 20:25-31).

When Joshua sensed that the sand in his hourglass was running low, he called the tribes to meet with him. The introduction to chapter 23 reads: "Now it came to pass, a long time after Yahweh had given rest to Israel from all their enemies round about, that Joshua was old.... And Joshua called for *all* Israel, for their elders, for their heads, for their judges, and for their officers."

Because chapters 23 and 24 are closely linked, it is possible that the meeting with the leaders of God's people took place in an open square within Shechem, whereas Joshua's meeting with all the people (chapter 24) probably took place in the natural amphitheater created by Mounts Ebal and Gerizim.

Encouragement of the Leaders, 23:1-8

Reminder of the Past, 23:3-4. A considerable period of time had elapsed since the events of the previous chapter. Joshua was now old.[1] The future well-being of the nation weighed heavily upon him. He felt the need to exhort the leaders of God's people to keep and do all that was written in the Book of the Law of Moses and to encourage them to drive out the nations that still remained in Canaan.

"And Joshua said to them: 'I am old, advanced in age. You have seen all that Yahweh your God has done to all these nations because of you, for Yahweh your God is He who has fought for you. See, I have divided to you by lot these nations that remain, to be an inheritance for your tribes, from the Jordan, with all the nations that I have cut off, as far as the Great Sea westward.' "

Joshua's words, "You have seen" reminded the people of their history. They had witnessed God roll back the waters of Jordan so that they could enter the land of Canaan; they had seen the walls of Jericho crumble before them; they had observed how God gave the people of Ai into their

---

1. Josephus, *Antiquities of the Jews* (V:1:117) believes that Joshua spent 40 years as a slave in Egypt, 40 years with Moses in the wilderness, and 25 years as Israel's commander following the death of Moses. He died at 110. It is evident from this chapter that Joshua, even though retired, was still in touch with the affairs of his people.

hand and then crushed both the southern and northern alliances; and they had participated in possessing houses and lands as God had promised (Deuteronomy 6:10-11).

God had been good to them, and they were to remember all that He had done.

It is in this area of remembering our past blessings that we are often most lax. Our society is obsessed with the future: the next upgrade of computer software, the five-year and ten-year forecasts of our company, where we will go for our next vacation, the colleges our children will attend, and what we will do in our retirement. There is nothing wrong with planning ahead, but we should also remember the way in which the Lord has led us. Joshua's words to the leaders of his people called upon them to remember all that God had done in the past, lest they lose sight of all His blessings.

One convenient way for us to stay in touch with what the Lord has done for us is to keep a journal. In this journal we can enter our prayer requests with the date on one page, and our praises for His answer on the other. I recall how some of my prayers begun in young adulthood were only answered forty years later. But they were answered ... abundantly!

Promise for the Future, 23:5. From dealing with God's help in the past Joshua moved to speak of the future. "And Yahweh your God will expel the people who remain in the land from before you and drive them out of your sight. So you shall possess their land, as Yahweh your God promised you." To understand God's plan and purpose we need to know His Word. There is no substitute for a personal knowledge of what He has chosen to reveal. From our knowledge of Scripture we receive guidance so that we can avoid the many pitfalls of life (cf. Psalm 119).[2]

God does not promise us limitless success in the secular sense of the word, but He does assure us that He will meet all our needs and sustain us throughout our lives.

Challenge for the Present, 23:6-8. So where does this leave us? The challenge of the present is to reorder our priorities, commit ourselves to meditate on a portion of God's Word each day, and follow wherever He may lead us. Note Joshua's words: "Therefore be very courageous to keep and to do all that is written in the Book of the Law of Moses, lest you turn aside from it to the right hand or to the left, and lest you go among these nations that remain among you. You shall not make mention of the name of their gods, nor cause anyone to swear by them; you shall not serve them nor bow down to them, but you shall hold fast to Yahweh your God, as you have done to this day."

Obedience to the Lord permits no compromise. The Israelites to whom Joshua spoke would find it tempting to dabble in the religious beliefs of the pagans. Some might excuse such interest by saying, "After all, what harm is there in knowing what they believe? It doesn't mean that I'm going to convert and become one of them! They have

---

2. To guide believers in their study of the Bible reference can be made to two books: *Unlocking the Scriptures* (Eugene, OR: Wipf & Stock, 2002), 224pp., and *Best Books for Your Bible Study Library* (Eugene, OR: Wipf & Stock, 2002), 95pp.

such interesting festivals, and appear so happy. I'd like to find out more about them." The subtleties of paganism are such that it is easy to be seduced by their supposed superior wisdom or drawn into the "liberty" (i.e., sensuality) of their lifestyle.

To stand against such allurements requires courage and a commitment to follow the Lord no matter how tempting or attractive these beliefs may appear on the surface.

Admonition in Light of the Past and the Future, 23:9-13

As with all good speakers Joshua summed up what he had been saying before he offered them encouragement to offset any fears they may have had: "For Yahweh has driven out great and strong nations from before you; and as for you, no man has stood before you to this day. One of your men puts to flight a thousand, for Yahweh your God is He who fights for you, just as He promised you. So take diligent heed to yourselves to love Yahweh your God."

Then Joshua gave them a solemn warning: "For if you ever go back and cling to the rest of these nations, these which remain among you, and intermarry with them, so that you associate with them and they with you, know with certainty that Yahweh your God will not continue to drive these nations out from before you; but they will be a snare and a trap to you, and a whip on your sides and thorns in your eyes, until you perish from off this good land which Yahweh your God has given you."

This was no empty rhetoric. There were many among the leaders of Israel who remembered the harsh treatment they had received at the hands of the Egyptian taskmasters. The last thing they wanted was to again be compelled to endure forced labor and cruel, unreasonable treatment.

But were Joshua's words what they could expect from a loving God? How could He promise both blessings and curses in the same breath? This dilemma has led some modern theologians to drive a wedge between the Old and New Testaments. They portray the God of the Old Testament as disinterested in His people's well-being, who becomes capricious when aroused. They also like to point to His merciless judgments whenever there are the slightest infractions of His legal code. According to these misguided proponents of Scripture it is only in the New Testament that we come across a God of love. Both views are wrong. God is not a passive-aggressive deity. His will is plain. It is our responsibility to know and follow what He has revealed. Those who obey Him are blessed. Those who deliberately disobey Him inevitably are punished.

Farewell to the Leaders, 23:14-16.

The leaders of the people may have been anticipating what came next. "Now behold, today I am going the way of all the earth, and *you know in all your hearts and in all your souls that not one word of all the good words which Yahweh your God spoke concerning you has failed*; all have been fulfilled for you, not one of them has failed" (emphasis added).

What fidelity! Joshua could face the end of his life with devotion so strong that even as the shadows began to gather about him his thoughts were of the Lord and what was best for his people. But note that he did not speak of what was going to happen to him. He directed the attention of the leaders to the One who is always faithful, who had not failed them, and who had fulfilled all the promises He had made to them!

This would have been a comfortable note on which Joshua could have ended his message. He, however, was not a pusillanimous leader who only spoke consoling words to his people. As amiable as his words of assurance were, his warning to the leaders to remain faithful to the Lord was grounded in reality. "It shall come about that just as all the good words which Yahweh your God spoke to you have come upon you, so Yahweh will bring upon you all the threats, until He has destroyed you from off this good land which Yahweh your God has given you. When you transgress the covenant of Yahweh your God, which He commanded you, and go and serve other gods and bow down to them, then the anger of Yahweh will burn against you, and you will perish quickly from off the good land which He has given you."

There was no room for misunderstanding. The Lord is a good and gracious Sovereign, but He does not tolerate the willful rebellion of His people (Psalm 78:36-37). There is a big difference, however, between God's discipline and His judgment. His discipline is designed to bring us to repentance. His judgment is often final.

John Newton was a man who knew God's discipline. He was a midshipman in the British Navy. When he tried to desert his ship, he was captured in West Africa, flogged and degraded. He eventually became the slave of a white slave trader's black wife. She humiliated him, and for years he lived a hungry and destitute life. All the while the Lord was dealing with him and causing him to long for peace and assurance of his eternal well-being. He was able to get a letter to his father who bought his freedom. The ship he sailed on for England was beset by a terrific storm, and nearly sank. For Newton this became the means that turned his thoughts Godward. He gave his life to Christ. His conversion was real. He began studying the Bible in addition to Greek, Hebrew, and Syriac, and he eventually entered the ministry. For the next forty-three years he labored faithfully for the Lord.

John Newton's legacy includes a hymn book that contains such hymns as "Glorious Things of Thee are Spoken," and "How Sweet the Name of Jesus Sounds." Though wayward in his early life, the Lord's discipline brought him to a place of surrender to the love and grace of a loving Father. He found that those who obey God's Word are blessed beyond anything they could ask or think, and those who attended John Newton's ministry found this to be a glorious reality.

CHAPTER 16

JOSHUA'S FAREWELL MESSAGES

Part Three

JOSHUA 24:1-33

The closing chapters of the book of Joshua contain three messages, each one longer than the one before it. A close look at these addresses reveals that although they were spoken to different groups of people they emphasize the same point, namely, the need for God's people to be faithful to Him and obey His revealed will. The central thrust of chapter 24 is found in verses 14 and 15:

"Now, therefore, fear Yahweh and serve Him in sincerity and truth; and put away the gods which your fathers served beyond the River [i.e., the Euphrates] and in Egypt, and serve Yahweh. If it is disagreeable in your sight to serve Yahweh, choose for yourselves today whom you will serve: whether the gods which your fathers served which were beyond the River, or the gods of the Amorites in whose land you are living; but *as for me and my house, we will serve Yahweh.*"

What God Has Done, 24:1-13

Joshua had gathered all the tribes of Israel together to Shechem. The Tabernacle had been brought up from

Shiloh, and all the people presented themselves before the Lord. As Joshua began his address, he was conscious of speaking for the Lord. He said, "Thus says Yahweh, the God of Israel." Then beginning with Abraham and his family when they lived in Ur of the Chaldeans near the Persian Gulf, he reminded the people of Israel that Abraham and his family had at one time served pagan gods (24:2; cf. Genesis 15:7; Nehemiah 9:7). But how did Abraham come to believe in the Lord so that he is known to posterity as the "father of the faithful"?

The answer is in 24:3, "Then I took your father Abraham ...." God intervened. But how? We need to turn to Acts 7:2 for an explanation of Abraham's conversion. There we read that "the God of glory" appeared to him. We have an indication of what this must have been like when we consider Acts 9:3-5. In all probability the Second Member of the Trinity appeared to him. His face shone with light brighter than the sun, and His intrinsic holiness emanated from His being (cf. Hebrews 1:3; see also Matthew 17:2).

Abraham knew that none of the gods he worshiped could compare with such splendor (i.e., glory), power, and inherent holiness. He did not need a long polemic on the fallacies of idolatry to convince him of the uniqueness of the One who had appeared to him. His response was immediate. He yielded himself without reservation to the Lord of glory, and this encounter changed his entire life. And his testimony to what he had seen impacted his family as well.

At the time God appeared to Abraham He made a threefold promise to him. It involved a land (Canaan), a seed (posterity), and national and universal blessing (Genesis 12:1-3). And now, as the descendants of Abraham look about them, they have tangible evidence that He has fulfilled His promise (Joshua 24:3-4).

As we consider 24:3-13, we should take note of the number of times the Lord refers to Himself in the first person:

"Then *I took* your father Abraham from beyond the River, and *[I] led* him through all the land of Canaan, and *[I] multiplied* his descendants and gave him Isaac. To Isaac *I gave* Jacob and Esau, and to Esau *I gave* Mount Seir to possess it; but Jacob and his sons went down to Egypt. Then *I sent* Moses and Aaron, and *I plagued* Egypt by what *I did* in its midst; and afterward *I brought* you out. *I brought* your fathers out of Egypt, and you came to the sea; and Egypt pursued your fathers with chariots and horsemen to the Red Sea. But when they cried out to [Me], *I put* darkness between you and the Egyptians, and brought the sea upon them and covered them; and your own eyes saw what *I did* in Egypt. And you lived in the wilderness for a long time. Then *I brought* you into the land of the Amorites who lived beyond the Jordan, and they fought with you; and *I gave* them into your hand, and you took possession of their land when *I destroyed* them before you. Then Balak the son of Zippor, king of Moab, arose and fought against Israel, and he sent and summoned Balaam the son of Beor to curse you. But *I was not willing* to listen to Balaam. So he had to bless you, and *I delivered* you from his hand. You crossed the Jordan and came to Jericho; and the citizens of Jericho fought against you, and the Amorite and the Perizzite and the Canaanite and the Hittite and the Girgashite, the Hivite and the Jebusite. Thus *I gave* them into your hand. Then *I sent* the hornet before you and it drove out the two kings of the Amorites from before you, but not by your sword or your bow. *I gave* you a land on which you had not labored, and cities which you had not built, and you have lived in them; you are eating of vineyards and olive groves which you did not plant."

The point is obvious. The Lord had cared for His people throughout their history!

This reminds me of my early years as a Christian. I had come to faith in Christ in my late teens, but I did not know how involved God was in my life. I felt very insecure. I prayed about the many problems I faced, but lacked confidence that the Lord heard and would answer my prayers. Now, as I look back on my life I see how at every stage the Lord was present to help and sustain me (cf. Deuteronomy 33:27).

In recounting the history of the family of Isaac's son, Jacob, God reminded the people of their sojourn in Egypt. There were probably some among them who, though now old, remembered the suffering they had endured when they lived in the "land of the Nile." But even their long-term residence in Egypt did not cause God to forget His people. Far from disregarding them, He used their stay in Egypt to multiply them into a great nation.

When the oppression of His people neared its end, the Lord sent Moses and Aaron to lead them out of bondage

(24:5-7). Then the Lord broke the power of Egypt by drowning Pharaoh's army in the Red Sea. He had miraculously parted the waters of the sea so that His people passed safely through it, but when the Egyptians tried to follow them the waters suddenly closed over them and Pharaoh's army was drowned.

It is also interesting to note that the years Israel spent in the desert are passed over without mention.

The next phase of God's work on behalf of His people involved their conquests in Transjordan (24:8-10; Numbers 21:21-35). Their victories over Sihon and Og were momentous feats, and yet God mentions it as if all He needed do was remind them of this part of their history.

These triumphs prepared the way for God's gracious acts in giving the land of Canaan to His people (24:11-13). He reminded them that they had crossed the Jordan and encircled the city of Jericho whose impregnable walls had fallen down. The citizens of Jericho had fought against them, but they had been defeated. The capture of Jericho was followed by wars with the Amorites, the Perizzites, the Canaanites, the Hittites, the Girgashites, the Hivites and the Jebusites. "And I gave them into your hand. Then I sent the hornet before you and it drove out the two kings of the Amorites from before you, but not by your sword or your bow."

The Lord had made mention of the first battle in which Israel was involved in Canaan. He then listed seven nations that fought against them, but none gained the mastery over them. The land occupied by these nations was given to His people, thus fulfilling His earlier promise that He would give them land on which they had not labored, and cities which they had not built, and the fruit of vineyards and olive groves which they had not planted.

A question naturally arises over the reference to the *sir'a*, "hornet" in verse 12 (cf. Exodus 23:28). The word *sir'a* means "downcast" or "discouraged." The late Dr. John Garstang claimed that the symbol of a bee or a hornet was used by the Egyptians to indicate the power of Pharaoh. If this view is adopted then Pharaoh's army would have had to wage war against the Canaanites before God's people left Egypt. If so, then this foray had weaken the people of Canaan.[1] If, however, the usage is figurative, then it would be a metaphor for the terror or panic the inhabitants experienced when their hearts became like water.[2] Hornets are not mentioned in the descriptions of the battles that took place (cf. 10:11), and so we are left to conjecture that the use is figurative and describes the fear that rendered the Amorites and their cohorts virtually powerless.

Response of the People, 24:14-28.

Joshua now began to move toward the institution of a covenant he wanted the people to make with the Lord. Bible scholars have compared these verses with ancient Near Eastern treaties.[3] Some are parity treaties (i.e., between equals) while others are suzerainty treaties (i.e.,

---

1. Garstang, *Joshua-Judges*, 258-60.
2. E. Neufeld, *Orientalia* 49 (1980), 30-57.

between a sovereign and his vassals). We find in Hittite suzerainty treaties that the first obligation laid upon a vassal was the prohibition of foreign alliances. And here the first obligation of the covenant between Israel and the Lord is a rejection of all foreign relations--i.e., with other gods, and with other political groups. This primary duty was required of Israel by Joshua (24:14-15, 23), and the record of the acceptance of this covenant-obligation by the people is interposed in the text for the sake of brevity.

The covenant called upon Israel to "fear" the Lord and "serve Him in sincerity[4] and truth"(24:14). The "fear of the Lord" is one of the most important and most neglected teachings of the Bible. It implies living ones life in "reverential awe" of God (cf. Hosea 3:5)–having respect for His infinite power, fear of offending Him and incurring His displeasure, submission to His authority, and recognition of the fact that His all-seeing eye sees everything that transpires on the earth.

Joshua followed up this invitation to "fear the Lord" by calling for a decision.[5] All present were asked to choose

---

3. Cf. Butler, *Joshua*, 257-61, 266-69; G. E. Mendenhall, *Biblical Archaeologist*, 17 (1954), 50-76.
4. The word is *tamim* and means "fullness," "completeness," "integrity." It looks at the congruence that should exist between a person's outward acts and his inner disposition.
5. See Butler, *Joshua*, 273-74. The uniqueness of Joshua's offer can best be understood when one considers that it was normally God who did the choosing. Here, however, the people are asked to choose their loyalties.

whom they would serve. His emphasis on "today" required an immediate response. A delay would only dull the sensitivity of the people. They have had clearly presented to them the contrast between "the gods whom their fathers served" and the Lord who had done great and mighty deeds on their behalf. Now they have to decide to whom they will give their allegiance.

A leader must lead by example, and Joshua boldly stated that as for him and his house, they would serve the Lord (24:15). He knew that the people had household idols in their possession (cf. Amos 5:26), and from his choice of words it appears as if he was aware of the fact that this was a common practice (cf. Genesis 31:19, 32, 34-35; 35:2, 4; cf. Deuteronomy 31:16; 32:16). He did not want them to think that these idols could coexist with trust in the Lord of glory.

The situation of the people of Israel illustrates for us how easy it is to go through the external routines and rituals of our religious faith, and yet have within our hearts those things that we cherish even though we know that they are wrong. From time to time we need some faithful servant of the Lord to remind us of the "idols" in our lives for, as Dr. William Blaikie has pointed out, "what honest and earnest heart does not feel that there are idols and images among ourselves that interfere with God's claims and God's glory as much as [the household idols] of the Israelites did?"[6]

Apparently Joshua's words to the people of Israel produced the desired result (24:16-18). "They answered and

---

6. Blaikie, *Joshua*, 395.

said, 'Far be it from us that we should forsake Yahweh to serve other gods; for Yahweh our God is He who brought us and our fathers up out of the land of Egypt, from the house of bondage, and who did these great signs in our sight and preserved us through all the way in which we went and among all the peoples through whose midst we passed. Yahweh drove out from before us all the peoples, even the Amorites who lived in the land. We also will serve Yahweh, for He is our God.'"

Joshua no more believed in "easy 'believism'" than those of us in Christian ministry do today. He pressed them to determine the depth of their sincerity. His voice must have been very firm as he stressed God's nature by adding, "He is a jealous God; He will not forgive your transgressions nor your sins. If you forsake Yahweh and serve foreign gods, then He will turn and do you harm and consume you, after He has done you good " (24:19-20).

The people's response was unequivocal, "No, but we will serve Yahweh" (24:21).

With this proof of the people's sincerity Joshua led the people as they entered into a formal covenant with the Lord. But first he insisted that they carry out their resolve by putting away all foreign gods, no matter how ornate and regardless of the promises of prosperity and blessing that was supposed to accompany their worship. To this further admonition the people responded, "We will serve Yahweh our God and we will obey His voice" (24:24).

Joshua recorded their words in the book of the law of God, and it was placed with the writings of Moses in the sanctuary. He also inscribed their words on a stone and placed it under an oak tree that was by the sanctuary.[7] This stone constituted a witness to all reminding them of what had taken place that day. And every time an Israelite's child inquired about the significance of the stone his godly father could tell him about the Lord and what He had done.

Covenants were transactions invested with special significance by people in the ancient Near East. They were looked upon as binding agreements, and the party that broke the agreement incurred a very severe penalty. The covenant entered into on that day obligated Israel to obey God's laws and honor Him in all things.

Joshua then dismissed the people. Each went to his own inheritance, and Joshua returned to Timnath-serah. The historian records the lasting effects of this convocation: "Israel served Yahweh all the days of Joshua and all the days of the elders who survived Joshua, and had known all the deeds of the Lord which He had done for Israel" (24:31).

End of An Era, 24:29-33

One of a pastor's many duties is to lay to rest those who have died. He also has the responsibility of comforting those who have been left behind and point unsaved loved

---

7. A large stone, dating from this period of Israelite history, has been found at Shechem, and many scholars believe it to be the stone mentioned here.

ones to Christ as the only hope of salvation. As this chapter comes to a close, the biblical historian records three burials.

Joshua's Burial, 24:29-31. "It came about after these things that Joshua the son of Nun, *the servant of Yahweh*, died, being one hundred and ten years old. And they buried him in the territory of his inheritance in Timnath-serah, which is in the hill country of Ephraim, on the north of Mount Gaash" (emphasis added).

After many years of faithful service Joshua had earned the right to be called "the servant of the Lord"–the highest title that can be bestowed on any person! And he was laid to rest with reverence and the acknowledgment of all that he had done for the nation.

On the wall of a hospice that I visit as occasion requires, there is a beautiful picture of the Tetons in Wyoming, and underneath the picture are these words:

> God saw that he was getting tired and a cure was not to be,
> So He put His arms around him and whispered,
> "Come home with me."
> With tearful eyes we watched him suffer
> And saw him fade away,
> Although we loved him dearly, we could not make him stay.
> –Anonymous

Joshua set the people of his day (and those of succeeding generations) a remarkable example of godly sincerity and loyal service. When he entered into his rest, the impact of his life was such that the people continued to serve the Lord for several years to come.

Joseph's Burial, 24:32. The second burial was Joseph's. "Now they buried the bones of Joseph, which the sons of Israel brought up from Egypt, at Shechem, in the piece of ground which Jacob had bought from the sons of Hamor the father of Shechem for one hundred pieces of money; and they became the inheritance of Joseph's sons."

This verse takes us back to Joseph's administration in Egypt (Genesis 50:24-25; Exodus 13:19). He, too, had been faithful in his service of the Lord. He believed strongly in God's promise to give Israel the land of Canaan for their inheritance, and to show where his loyalties lay he instructed his brothers to carry his coffin out of Egypt and bury it in the portion of ground his father had bought at Shechem (Genesis 33:19). And though centuries had intervened since Joseph's death, his wishes were carried out. In the resurrection he will claim a portion of Canaan as his inheritance (cf. Daniel 12:2).

Eleazar's Burial, 24:33. "And Eleazar the son of Aaron died; and they buried him at Gibeah of Phinehas his son, which was given him in the hill country of Ephraim." Eleazar's death removed from the leadership of Israel another stalwart. His place would be taken by his son, Phineas. The respect shown Eleazar at the time of his death is evident from the fact that he, too, was held to be an honorable man.

As we look about us and take note of the servants of the Lord who have been taken from us, we cannot help but exclaim with David,

> Help, LORD, for the godly man ceases to be,
> For the faithful disappear from among the sons of men.
> They speak falsehood to one another;
> With flattering lips and with a double heart they speak.
> May the LORD cut off all flattering lips,
> The tongue that speaks great things;
> Who have said, "With our tongue we will prevail;
> Our lips are our own; who is lord over us?"
> (Psalm 12:1-4 NASB).

The diminishing ranks of the godly men and women seems to be filled with those whose skill is comprised of subtle deception and flattery, with scarcely a thought for truth and honesty in their dealings with others. May it be our aim to live for the Lord as Joshua had done so that when we die we may have impacted the lives of others with the truth!

www.ingramcontent.com/pod-product-compliance
Lightning Source LLC
Chambersburg PA
CBHW060607230426
43670CB00011B/2003